POETRY COMPI

C000318728

GREAT MINDS

From Derbyshire

Edited by Heather Killingray

 Young**Writers**

First published in Great Britain in 2005 by:
Young Writers
Remus House
Coltsfoot Drive
Peterborough
PE2 9JX
Telephone: 01733 890066
Website: www.youngwriters.co.uk

SB ISBN 1 84460 876 X

Foreword

This year, the Young Writers' 'Great Minds' competition proudly presents a showcase of the best poetic talent selected from over 40,000 up-and-coming writers nationwide.

Young Writers was established in 1991 to promote the reading and writing of poetry within schools and to the youth of today. Our books nurture and inspire confidence in the ability of young writers and provide a snapshot of poems written in schools and at home by budding poets of the future.

The thought, effort, imagination and hard work put into each poem impressed us all and the task of selecting poems was a difficult but nevertheless enjoyable experience.

We hope you are as pleased as we are with the final selection and that you and your family continue to be entertained with *Great Minds From Derbyshire* for many years to come.

Contents

Hope Valley College

Lady Manners School

Landau Forte College

Lauren Hughes (11)	68
Christopher Griffiths (11)	69
Stacey Hyndman (13)	69
Monique Foster (11)	70
Melissa Archer (11)	70
Emily Watson (11)	71
Andrew Dean (13)	72
Hannah Cooper (13)	72
Paris Sullivan (13)	73
Matthew Swain (11)	73
Sophie Porter (13)	74
Michelle Hill (13)	74
Olivia Smith (11)	75
Ben Wilton (13)	76
Chris Thomas (13)	77
Kate Patterson (11)	77
Daniel Bown (11)	78
Jack Smith (11)	78
Gurveer Singh Hansi (14)	79
Hannah Nichols-Green (12)	79
Silpa Gembali (12)	80
Sarah Allsopp (13)	80
Laura Maskrey (12)	81
Tamika Short (12)	81
Ann-Marie Hitchcock (12)	82
Sam Gandy (12)	82
Jordan Britton (11)	83
Navdeep Kaur Johal (12)	83
Charlton Kent (12)	84
Kathryn Loveless (11)	84
Ryan Joyce (11)	85
Gareth Povey (11)	85
Parveen Kaur Thandi (11)	86
Timothy Riley (11)	86
Elicia Redfern (11)	87
Taraseen Iqbal (11)	87
Kelly-Ann Hutchinson (11)	88
Dean Fletcher (11)	88
Peter Temple (11)	89
Thomas Roethenbaugh (11)	89

Kaylie Scattergood (14)	90
Kirsty Tomlinson (12)	90
Hayley Gaskin (14)	91
Lewis Aldridge (13)	92
Katy Heap (12)	92
Kalisha Hamilton (12)	93
Stephanie Fox (12)	94
Sam West (11)	94
Jordan Kelly (11)	95
Ellis Hannah Thorpe (11)	96
Joseph Thorpe (11)	97
Mark Woodward (12)	97
Frances Martin (12)	98
Tom Buckner (11)	98
Heather Dobbs (11)	99
Anna Kingwell (12)	99
Michael Wood (11)	100
Hafizah Khatoon (11)	101
Jagraaj Dhammi (13)	102
James Capps (11)	103
Raheela Hussain (12)	103
Rose Akers (14)	104
Danielle Randle (11)	104
David Wilson (10)	105
Connor Boylan (11)	105
Aisha Roberts (11)	106
Cassandra Duncan (11)	106
Jagjeevan Johal (11)	107
Taibah Yasin (11)	108

Netherthorpe School
Lucy Stanton-Greenwood (16)	109
Jody Robinson (15)	110

Noel-Baker Community School & Language College
Johnathan Curd (13)	111
Samantha Kemp (12)	112
Shellie Morgan (12)	112
Zoe Handley (12)	113
Becky Keeling-Brown (12)	114
Catherine Huynh (12)	114

Simon Murney (14)   135
Daniel Schurian (15)   136
Ian Wallis (14)   136
Jessica Munton (14)   137
Chantelle Morris (15)   137
Ashley Pipes (14)   137
Leonard Dolby (14)   138
Flora Solomou (14)   138

St John Houghton RC School, Ilkeston
Jacob King (11)   139

The Ecclesbourne School
Leigh Davies (11)   139
Joe Hoblyn (12)   140
Isabel Fleming (11)   140
Alice Lowe (12)   141
Charlie Pollard (11)   141
Bethanie Ragsdell (12)   142
Christopher Watts (11)   142
Claire Cooper (12)   143
Katherine Curley (12)   144
Connor Rogers (12)   145
Zack Oxley (12)   145
Elizabeth Wright (12)   146
Mark Shepherd (12)   146
Rosalyn Smith (12)   147
James Smith (11)   148

The Hucknall National School
Rosie Dodd (12)   148
Matthew Burton (12)   149
Alison Stones (13)   149
Georgia Noon (12)   150
Allan Ndiweni (11)   150
Isabel Roe (12)   151
Natalie Jowett (15)   151
Daniel Walton (11)   152
Jacob Cole (11)   152
Lucie Mann (12)   153

The Meadows Community School

The Poems

Happy I Ams!

I am,
I am,
A souvenir, so I know that I've been here,
Winning the lottery all the time,
I've got to think of happy things to make a rhyme,
I am,
I am,
A happy filled recycled can,
Peace and happiness across the countries from here to Japan,
I am,
I am,
A chocolate sweet,
So all the kiddies can eat, eat, eat,
A flower, a teddy bear
Spreading goodness everywhere,
I am,
I am,
A relationship,
A friendship,
I am,
I am, what?

Anthony Needham (12)
Da Vinci Community College

The World

The news is driving me up the wall
the world can be a horrid place,
it's like a ticking bomb ready to go off
and part of it already has.

But despite the horror and pain
people are getting closer together
and the world is getting a better place,
and hopefully the world will unite as one.

Katie Hogan (12)
Da Vinci Community College

Sad I Ams!

I am . . .
A hot air balloon
That goes so high in the sky
It can reach the clouds
And reach the sun
And can fly so high, so high.
I am . . .
A sunshine
On top of a bright white cloud
Floating around
On the ground
And clouds in the sky being surrounded.
I am . . .
A boy
Who's locked up in his room
In the dark
It's so, so quiet
Hopefully I will be out soon.
I am . . .
A pen
A red, bright pen
Who writes all day.
In some hay
I am a red, bright pen.

Grant Nunns (12)
Da Vinci Community College

I Am

I am . . .
a snake biting its first prey,
a monkey playing its first play.

I am . . .
a little ant feeling depressed,
me feeling stressed.

Drew Wilson (12)
Da Vinci Community College

I Am . . . Loved!

I am . . .
A cute puppy
That's a few years old
A knight with friends
That's brave and bold
A ray of hope
When the Earth is cold.

I am . . .
The one that's turned to
When a child is in need
A tiny but lovely
Little seed
The rider riding
Upon his steed.

I am . . .
A new world
Waiting to be found
The heart of all the children
That make the world spin round.

Vanessa Alliss (12)
Da Vinci Community College

Sad I Am

I am . . .
A burst ball lying in a bin.
A frog with no legs.
A fish with no tail.
I am . . .
The leftover bones from a Sunday dinner.
A rusty bike abandoned in a pond.
A bird with no wings.
I am . . .
Helpless!

Stuart Sharman (12)
Da Vinci Community College

What Is It?

It's not a disease, you can't catch it.
It affects four percent of the population.
Like an invisible sheet that reappears when it wants to.

Some people don't have it,
Some people glaze over when you mention it.
It's like an award only given to some people.
The government refuse to believe that it exists,
Ignoring it as if it were a stranger in the street.

Scientists think it's the way the brain's wired,
The Greeks knew about it, they named it.
It's classed as a learning disability.

Some people are scared to admit they have it, others think it's a gift.
It's classed as a dirty word in the education system.
People who have it tend to be very creative
Almost like geniuses in their own field.
It can't be cured.

It affects the way a person learns
Like a broken leg stops a dog from walking.

Famous people have it, it never held them back.
It's so common, it's like leaves falling off a tree,
Brown leaves, red leaves.
It affects every person in a different way.
We created it ourselves when we were very young.

I have it, my sister has it, but we don't let it stop us.

Have you guessed what it is yet!

It's *dyslexia*.

Malcolm John Baker (15)
Da Vinci Community College

Sad I Ams

I am . . .
The top,
Of an empty bottle of pop,
The scratchings
From an empty yoghurt pot,
The useless arm
From last year's Barbie doll.
I am . . .
A letter,
Of which the writing has vanished.
The pen
Where you can't find the end,
The tongueless stapler, springless,
The dog clip,
The dried up watered envelope,
That Mars instead of Snickers,
The stamped addressed reply,
That you forgot
To deliver.

Nicole Hennessy (12)
Da Vinci Community College

My Poem

The hot air balloon Da Vinci
Flies through the sky
Carrying the happy people.
Just starting out in life
A newly married couple
On their honeymoon today
The balloon feels safe
With people to protect
The weather gets warmer
As the balloon rises about the clouds.
Letting the sun smile upon the couple
Onwards the colourful rainbow cruises . . .

Leanne Sheldon (12)
Da Vinci Community College

Happy I Am!

I am . . .
A beautiful horse
With silk-black fur.
A river
That calmly flows.
A lion
Running gracefully.
I am . . .
A dolphin
Making people smile.
A moon that makes a silver sky.
I am . . .
The smile
On your face.
A tadpole
With a flowing tail.
I am . . .
A helping hand
Stopping you from falling.
A flower
With the sweetest scent.

Emma Tooby (12)
Da Vinci Community College

Angry I Ams!

I am . . .
A storm
Brewing over a town.
A bomb
Waiting to explode.

I am . . .
A lion woken
By a stampede.
A fish
Caught by the fisherman.

Samantha Cregan (12)
Da Vinci Community College

Sad I Ams!

I am . . .
The choice
That no one chooses.
I am . . .
The rain
That everyone hates.
I am . . .
A rusty door
That no one dares open.
I am . . .
An injured kitten
That no one wants to help.
I am . . .
The mud
On your shoes.
I am . . .
An ancient mummy
That everyone had forgot.

Victoria Reader (12)
Da Vinci Community College

I Am . . .

I am . . .
The sun.
A flower that hasn't grown yet.
The stars at night shining bright.
A daffodil growing in the spring.
I am . . .
A butterfly way up high.
A rocket reaching for the stars.
A light shining bright.
The sunrise.
The moon glowing in the night's sky.

Natasha Moore
Da Vinci Community College

Sad I Ams

I am . . .
The mud
On the bottom of your new shoes.
The scraps of bacon
That no one seems to like.
I am . . .
One choice
That never gets chosen.
The nutritional information on the back of a can
That no one ever reads.
The three leaf clover
Amongst all others.
I am . . .
The wilting flower
At the back of your garden.
The chewing gum on your trousers
Fresh and fully hardened.
That desire
That can never be met.

Kaysha Wallis (12)
Da Vinci Community College

I Ams

I am . . .
A bike
That no one ever uses.
A computer
That needs a lead.
I am . . .
A TV
That needs tuning.
A chair
That keeps on breaking.

Carl Moss (12)
Da Vinci Community College

Happy I Ams

I am . . .
The sun
High up in the sky.
A chick
Waiting to be hatched.
A puppy
Getting my treats.
I am . . .
A princess
Waiting to be crowned.
A young baby
Having my first Christmas.
A colourful fish
Swimming in the sea.
A cat
Getting my food.
A human
Winning the lottery.
A rainbow
Colourful and bright
A pot of gold
In a millionaire's house.

Lauren Bates (12)
Da Vinci Community College

I Am . . .

A dolphin
that everyone loves.
A flower
as yellow as the sun.
A newborn baby.
A child on Christmas Day
unwrapping their presents,
waiting for the surprise
that's hidden inside.

Lisa-Marie Shaw (12)
Da Vinci Community College

The Egyptians

The Egyptians are a bit like . . .
Graffiti artists
Writing on the wall.
The Egyptians are a bit like . . .
Choreographers.
Parties through the night.
The Egyptians are a bit like . . .
Christians
Worshipping their god.
The Egyptians are a bit like . . .
Modern day architects
Building buildings as big as the Eiffel Tower.
The Egyptians are a bit like us,
Just 3,000 years old.

Rebecca Piggott (12)
Da Vinci Community College

Wynken, Blynken And Nod

Wynken, Blynken and Nod one night
Sailed off in a wooden shoe -
Sailed on a river of crystal light,
Into a sea of dew.
'Where are you going and what do you wish?'
The old moon asked the three.
'We have come to fish for the herring fish
That live in this beautiful sea;
Nets of silver and gold have we,'
Said Wynken, Blynken and Nod.

Jason Hawke (12)
Da Vinci Community College

Desert

The sun blazed in the sky
The sweat dripped off my chin
Sand blew in my eye
I was unhealthily thin.

I had been out here for days
I needed something to eat
My mind was just a haze
The sand burnt my bare feet.

My knees began to shake
My life flashed before me
I didn't know how much more I could take
I could hardly even see.

I heard something overhead
They had come to save me
I was an inch off being dead
I was free!

Joseph Davis (14)
Hasland Hall Community School

A Dog's Christmas

It's Christmas Eve
and all through the town children are sleeping peacefully.

It's cold and snowy and nobody cares
as we are locked in our kennels so bare and lonely
with no one there to donate a home for Christmas.

Every person that passes, just stops and stares as
we long for a home for this one and lonely Christmas.

A dog's for life
not just for Christmas.

Rachel Fox (15)
Hasland Hall Community School

Keep Skateboarding Alive

Pop, click, ting
These are most of the sounds of a beautiful sport,
All the wonders of the thought.

Its graphics are smooth and nice,
But, it comes at a heavy price.

My joy of skating over these years,
Conquering most of my fears.

Even the ollie is a piece of art,
Especially when it is high and looks smart.

Spinning a kickflip or two
And landing on a griptape like glue.

Some flips I will never hit
Like an impossible or a 540 flip.

I know now I shall not quit
Because I have to conquer that 540 flip.

Doing stairs is a thrill
3, 4, 5 or rolling down a hill.

A pop shove it is even a skill
Pop . . . shove . . . trying not to fall and spill.

Skateboarding is not a crime; it's an art
The crime is judging it as bad!

Thomas Fry (14)
Hasland Hall Community School

Nowhere To Run

Nowhere to run,
Nowhere to hide,
You're backed in a corner,
Your eyes shut tight.
The darkness is everywhere,
There's fear in your bones,
Your limbs are so stiff, nothing dares move.
Shadows are surrounding you,
Your heart beats fast,
The wind is howling like a racing dirt track.
There are faces you see haunting your sight,
You don't know where you're from or where you're going.
The adrenaline is being pumped swiftly through your veins.
Your head's all a blur,
Are you going insane?
Trees are all you see for miles and miles,
Then a bright light comes near,
And only a nightmare did you endure.

Kelly-Ann Harvey (14)
Hasland Hall Community School

Only One

You are not the only one
My heart has ever known,
Yours are not the only lips
That ever kissed my own,
But no one else in all my life
Has ever meant so much,
No one else could ever have
Your tender, loving touch.
The others are forgotten,
Which I really don't regret,
I only wish that you had been
The very first boy I met.

Lauren Clarke (12)
Hasland Hall Community School

Uncle Iestyn And Ali I Wish

I miss you,
It seems that you have been gone
For so long,
It may only be a few months or years,
But it seems forever.

I look to the stars
To look for Ali and you
But they don't talk back,
Just twinkle in the sky.

I miss you both, I want to see you again,
I wish that none of it
Had happened to Ali or you.

I miss you Ali, you are my special brother.

I wish you were alive
I wish you were here
I want you with me
I want you both now.

My special brother Ali
And my uncle Iestyn.

Jennie May (14)
Hasland Hall Community School

I Wish . . .

I wish . . .
I should be so lucky
To fall in love one day,
But whether that would happen or not
I'd be willing to pay.
I'd look into the future
To see what I could see
And hopefully I'd visualise my family and me.

Joanne Clay (14)
Hasland Hall Community School

Leaving My Dog

Today we went to buy a dog
But didn't expect it to be such a grog
Got him home, he didn't want to be alone
Even when left to chew a large bone.

When we went out he chewed the chair
And everywhere he left his hair
Total destruction followed him everywhere
What a sight we had to bear.

Half-chewed shoes and blobs of poo
Oh why can't he just use the loo?
How much time and how much cash
How much longer will he last?

Walking with the dog today
All he wanted to do was play
Let him off, he ran away
Now he's gone, I wish he'd stay.

Missing him, the place is clean
When through the window came a blue beam
There he was in the back,
The policeman had him in a sack.

Now he's back the place is a mess
But for now it's good I guess
Tomorrow is another day,
All my commands he will obey.

Eight weeks we tried to get it right
But now he has a harder bite.
In the garden he dug a hole
And chewed off the rubber round his bowl.

Enough's enough, he's got to go
Or we'll have no grass left to mow
We're sad he's gone but for today
We'll have to look forward to our cat called May.

Naomi Maqsood (11)
Hasland Hall Community School

The Simpsons

Bart Simpson is my kind of kid,
He's funny, he's stupid and sometimes he flips his lid.
Bart he sets cakes on the floor,
Homer dives down
And Bart takes his money, he takes it all.

Homer likes drinking,
His favourite beer is Duff,
His favourite food is doughnuts
And when he tries to run, it makes him huff and puff.

Maggie sucks her dummy,
And sometimes it is funny,
But she thinks it is yummy.

Lisa plays her saxophone,
But it makes Bart moan.

The kids like watching TV,
Their favourite show is Itchy and Scratchy,
This is about a cat and mouse,
Who chase each other around the house.

Krusty the clown,
He hasn't always got a frown.

Grandpa is a moaning old git,
And sometimes he gets a hit.

Moe runs the local bar,
Homer always goes in the car.

Jamie Platts (11)
Hasland Hall Community School

Come On Monty (Rap)

Come on Monty,
I'm counting on you,
Along with plenty of other people too.
I'm by your side, all the way,
Because you're going to win at the end of the day!

Monty, you're the best by far,
There'll be people cheering in every bar,
You'll get the best time,
While the rest are still down at the starting line.

So, come on Monty,
Win please,
It will be as easy as eating cheese.
Come on Monty don't delay,
Make sure that the other teams pay.

So Monty make me proud,
When you do I will shout out loud,
Cos I'll get a whole grand,
From the bookie, behind that stand.

On your marks, get set, go,
Monty hurry up, you're too slow,
And Gabby wins, the speakers say,
So it looks like I'm going to have to pay.

Camilla Eyley (11)
Hasland Hall Community School

My Rainbow

Red I love very much
A green crunchy apple
In a bright coloured scarf
Neptune in the salty sea
Blue rain in the sky
Orange like a leaf in autumn
And a huge *rainbow!*

Alice Redihough (11)
Hasland Hall Community School

Chance!

I have a horse called Chance,
And my goodness does he prance.
He's a dark bay and has a beautiful neigh!

He's got a long black mane and tail,
Can you imagine him,
My perfect male.

When I give him a mint,
He, he sort of gives me this hint.
He gobbles it up and says thank you.
But for me, it's time to pick up poo!

I tack him up and climb aboard
And gallop around, let people adore.

My pony - he's my best friend.
Now it's time to say bye, bye.
To the horse I love and I bet I will cry.

Kayleigh Walker (12)
Hasland Hall Community School

The Natural World

The stars glitter in the sky,
the clouds swiftly pass you by
all different types of flowers
the wind blows with all its power.

On the floor the grass lay,
people walk along the sandy bay,
animals running free and wild
with a happy, joyful child.

Fish swim down the stream,
blinded by the sun's beam,
the moon gleams all through the night
all this is a beautiful sight.

Danielle Sheppard (11)
Hasland Hall Community School

I Wish, I Wish

I wish, I wish
To be a golden fish,
How I wish to be a golden fish,
Swimming, swerving all day long,
Oh I wish.

I wish, I wish
To be a young deer
How I wish to be a young deer,
Prancing and dancing all day long,
Oh I wish.

I wish, I wish
To be a graceful butterfly,
How I wish to be a graceful butterfly,
Soaring and fluttering all day long,
Oh I wish.

I wish, I wish
I wish, I wish
How I wish to be . . .
What shall I wish for?

Marcia Paulucci (11)
Hasland Hall Community School

Dolphin Watching

Deep blue sea
Dolphin watching,
Swimming around
Up and down.
I wish it were me,
In amongst these graceful creatures.
To be free and wild
In the deep blue sea.
Moving gracefully through the surf,
Riding up on the crest of a wave.

Emma Haslam (14)
Hasland Hall Community School

Macey

Macey is so nice,
She eats red ice.
Macey's hair is brown,
The rain drips down.
Macey's eyes are green,
She has a scene.
Macey's clothes are pink,
She writes with blue ink.
Macey is so kind,
She sings in her mind.
Macey has some rings,
She thought it had wings.
Macey crossed the River Nile,
She can run a mile.
Macey knocked at the door,
She's nearly at the moor.
Macey crossed a bridge,
She put a yoghurt in the fridge.
Macey is so nice,
She eats red ice.
Macey, Macey you're the best,
So much better than the rest.

Demi Marie Turner (12)
Hasland Hall Community School

Footy

F ooty is my favourite sport,
O oh, aah, Cantona, you're my favourite super star
O ops, I missed a penalty,
T oo bad, they lost again.
Y eah! What a cracking goal.

Lewis Carter (12)
Hasland Hall Community School

Christmas

C are for others
H ave a great Christmas
R eally happy when you're opening presents
I love Christmas
S o enjoy Christmas
T he best day is Christmas Eve
M ore presents the happier you are
A nd have a great Christmas
S o your mum and dad haven't wasted any money.

Christmas is great
It's not second rate
Because it is great.

When you believe in Santa
Christmas is great
But if you don't
It's just not the same.

If you believe in Santa don't stay up
Because if your eyes shut for 5 seconds
The presents will be there
But if you see your mum and dad after 5 seconds
Well don't cry.

So he gives you presents
And sweets
No, he's not real
The man is your dad
And another thing Santa is really lazy.

Liam Griffin (11)
Hasland Hall Community School

My Teacher

Mrs Ryan, she is a very small, skinny lion.
Her beady, brown eyes are always looking at you,
She wants her students to do well in life.

She wears her gold and silver jewellery, jangly jewellery,
Always on her right arm, never her left.
Maybe she is mad, about jewellery,
She loves to wear the colour red,
Red on Wednesday, red on Tuesday.

Mr Ryan is a very caring, friendly lion,
Her long black straggly hair, tied up or down,
She looks like a funny clown.
Complete with her shiny red lipstick
Which makes her lips look big and bright.

Her teeth are so very white as snow and so very straight
No wonder, she's got a big cheesy grin!

April Allerton (14)
Hasland Hall Community School

The Zoo

The classroom was like a zoo!
Mad headed children shouted and said 'Boo!'
Pens and pencils being thrown across the room
And then the bookshelf went boom!
The anger escaped from the teacher
The teacher shouted, 'Silent!'
But the children just carried on!
Then the head teacher walked in . . .
And said, 'It's like a zoo in here,
I think I'll see you later!'
The bell rang and
All the monkeys had escaped from the zoo!

Katie Mitchell (12)
Hasland Hall Community School

Him And Her

There was an old man called John,
He has not got a girl because she has gone,
She ran off with a man,
She cooked him dinner in a pan,
What happened is he cheated on her,
So she cheated on him,
So that's that.
He got her a mat,
The girl he cheated with is Nat,
The boy she cheated with is Paul,
They did it in the hall,
She said she did not do it at all,
So John had a cup of tea,
He was very sad,
She was mad,
So that's the story of Balamory for today.

Sherelle Mellors (12)
Hasland Hall Community School

Saltergate

S ilence does not happen here,
A ll we do is cheer and jeer.
L et loose our enthusiastic thoughts,
T aunting the other side in their club shorts.
E ither by singing or chanting,
R aving or ranting!
G azing at the Spireites,
A ll are heroes in our sights.
T ogether Chesterfield is our team,
E very year the FA Cup is our dream!

Andrew Laming (12)
Hasland Hall Community School

Abortion

Today I started kicking Mummy,
I did that just for you,
Can't you see I need you Mummy,
I need you to help me through.

Please don't give me away Mummy,
See, I hear you rowing,
Please will you stop shouting, Mummy,
It's all too overpowering.

Even though I can't see you Mummy,
I love you more each day,
I want to be with you Mummy,
And that's the only way.

Can't I change your mind Mummy,
I promise I won't be a pain,
Can't you say you love me Mummy,
That's all that I obtain.

I don't know when I'm going Mummy,
I hope you change your mind,
I know that me and you Mummy,
We'll get on just fine.

Ouch! What you doing Mummy,
Stop! That hurts my arm,
Ouch! It's really hurting Mummy,
Please keep me safe from harm.

Mummy, I feel all funny,
I cannot feel my toes,
Mummy, I can't see properly,
Please don't let me go.

Stacey Nuttall (14)
Hasland Hall Community School

Nil-Nil

I've been sent to my room.
It's really boring.
I've unmade my bed,
Kicked the door in
And counted the squares
On the child-proof flooring.
I can just hear the match
But not who's scoring
And outside the miserable rain is pouring.
'You can come out now,' shouts Dad.
I ignore him
Because inside the miserable sulk is gnawing.
But I'm too cross to read
Or do a drawing,
So I creep down the stairs
And catch Man U scoring.
My heavy heart
I suddenly soaring.
Like the fans in the stands
We hold hands and start roaring.
We leap in the air
Call a truce to our warring.
So there we were roaring,
Hearts soaring,
About scoring . . .
When the ref decides . . .
It's offside!

Zoe McTigh (12)
Hasland Hall Community School

Friends!

Friends are always there for you,
They help you when you're down.
Friends never lie to you,
When you ask they don't frown.

Whether good or bad.
Friends will tell you everything,
The secrets and the gossip,
If it's about a lad.

A true friend is someone,
Who will do anything for you.
They will do it all year round,
Through, through and through.

A friend will come around,
When you need to talk.
They don't even moan,
If you want to take a walk.

Friends are very special,
In each and every way.
I wouldn't swap mine for the world,
Not even for a day!

Melanie Higgins (12)
Hasland Hall Community School

Hallowe'en

Hallowe'en, Hallowe'en
All people dressed up
Lots of houses they have been to
Lots of treats they have
On display is a pumpkin
Will he smile, or frown
Every child loves Hallowe'en
Every child loves treats
Noises of children having a good Hallowe'en.

Laurissa Marsden (12)
Hasland Hall Community School

The Cup Final Dream

It was a hot, sticky, airless day,
Not good weather in which to play.
As a team we were all psyched up,
It was the final of the league cup.
My heart was pounding like a drum,
My legs so tense, my feet were numb.
I came out of the changing rooms and looked at the crowd,
Everyone was cheering, it was really loud.
We got lined up, the whistle blew,
Down the pitch the ball flew.
The time was going really fast,
I was getting tired, half-time at last.
The score was 0-0, we needed a winner,
Our left-winger ran and did a great spinner.
It came off his boot onto my head,
Into the back of the net, leaving the keeper for dead.
The game had finished, we won 1-0,
To lift the cup was such a thrill.

Matt Bunting (12)
Hasland Hall Community School

My Friend

Standing by all the way.
Here to help you through your day.

Holding you up when you are weak.
Helping you find what it is you seek.

Catching your tears when you cry.
Pulling you through when the tide is high.

Absorbing your voice when you talk.
Standing by when you learn to walk.

Just being there through thick and thin.
I'll always be there to help you win.

Carly Andrews (13)
Hasland Hall Community School

Differences!

Most people in this world don't get on,
Because of religion, colour, terrorism and income.
Innocents and others die from people like this.
Adults and children scared out of their wits.
There's always talk about peace and no war,
But that's all it is, talk, nothing more.
Someone should do something about the whole thing.
Wait! It shouldn't be left to just one person,
Everyone should join in.
Maybe a protest, a parade, a meeting of some kind!
Opinion and state of mind
Nothing will ever work, not today, not tomorrow. *Never!*
No one can ever promise to stop war, fighting, racism and terrorism,
That's how life will be! *Forever!*

Hannah Smith (12)
Hasland Hall Community School

That's Life

Why do things go from bad to worse,
Especially when you're already down.
Nobody there to talk to
There are no smiles, just frowns.

Friendship, family or relationship problems,
Somehow we all get through,
The troubles of everyday life,
Troubles old or new.

At the end of the day be thankful,
That we've all got a life of our own,
Each unique in its own special way
And that we are here to be known.

Alex Wright (14)
Hasland Hall Community School

Gone Without A Trace

(I was inspired to write this poem by the loss of Jono)

She woke early this morning,
longing to see his face
but her heart sank quite quickly
see he had gone without a trace.

She cried until it hurt,
but it wouldn't change a thing,
she was alone and missed him badly,
held close to her was his ring.

She wanted to be by his side
but knew it was time for him to go,
alone he lay, lifeless and smiling
she figured time would go so slow.

She gave him one last kiss
and slowly walked away,
knowing she would never forget
this sad and gloomy day.

She knew her heart would hurt
and her loss would cause such pain,
but all their happy memories
would in her mind remain.

Tracey May (16)
Hasland Hall Community School

How To Do Your Homework

'Keep your hands off the table,' says Aunty Mabel.
'Don't underline in pen,' dictates Uncle Glen.
'Stop feeding it to the cat,' says Grandma Pat.
'Don't . . . screw it up and please don't stuff it in your cup.'
In the end I got a 4A!
And didn't listen to anything my family had to say . . .

Jack Allinson (12)
Hasland Hall Community School

Song Of The Falling Author

Speechless lyrics flutter
Bound to the foes of silence and death-like
Flight of traumatic full stops.
But does it all halt?
Does it end with the last gushing, soaring,
Sorrow-filled thought . . . the song of the
Near dead?
Written words phase out into the
Air . . . they disappear, they fizzle and fuse
Electrically away . . . they're lost to the
Grasses of woven past . . . entwined with the
Peace of natural forms.
Or does it begin? Do spoken waves wash to
New shores?
Only they will know what he once said . . . or
Is there existence after life's first
Breath?
The surrealism of creation proves that this
Is so . . . an exquisitely perfect eve for
Whoever looks beyond what they know,
Whoever conquers fear, doubts not the Lord,
But gives in to faith, trust and
Determination . . . undermining the evilness
Of falling to satanic death.
So what did the eagle cry? The eagle didn't
Cry. It smiled.

Chloë Warren (15)
Hasland Hall Community School

The Strings Of Life

Some say she tried too hard
Some say she tried too long
She always listened well
Listened to the magpie's song.

Her heart was cold and empty
She thought she lived on strings
The puppet, God controlled
Just wanted to grow wings.

She wanted to be free
And fly away into the moon
Vanish into the sun
Feel the warmth of the afternoon.

With a slip of a knife
A deep breath was at the end
Now that it was over
Everybody wished they'd been her friend.

Zoe Barraclough (12)
Hasland Hall Community School

Sun And Moon

The sun is like a golden bauble,
Hanging unsuspended forever glowing,
Its beauty will someday end,
For now we will delay and stop it from going.

The moon however is like an enlarged pearl,
With little bumps and scratches.
It takes its light from the sun,
Some things are bright but the moon has no matches.

The sun and moon will one day go,
But keep to the present and let things flow.

Sam Hull (12)
Hasland Hall Community School

A Better Place!

Ain't it funny
how life goes by
not many worries in our lives
we fall in and out of love all the time
but one mega thing in our world is *death!*
We try to prevent death
keep their souls in our lives
sometimes we do,
sometimes we don't,
we lose to a better place.
But we have to remember
we lose their cage, not their souls.
They're searching the world
waiting for us to join them
in this new heavenly world.

Shirlene Atkin (15)
Hasland Hall Community School

Don't Say Don't

Don't chew on your mother
Don't bite your brother
Don't suck on that lead
Don't eat your bed
Don't believe that stranger
Don't think about making any danger
Don't eat that wall
Don't make that lad fall
Don't drink the ink
Don't wear pink

Why do people say *don't* so much

Why don't they just say *do?*

Kieran Roach (12)
Hasland Hall Community School

The Seasons

Four seasons make up a calendar year,
Some we love, some we fear.
Each has something different to say,
To make each day differ in a funny way.

Summer is warm and dry and good
The sun shines daily just as it should.
People take holidays, eat ice cream and have fun
It makes people happy, that big round sun.

Autumn comes and the wind does blow
The rain it starts and continues to flow
The leaves from the trees, fall to the ground
And things like conkers can be found.

The snow falls, winter must be here
The dark nights is something we all fear,
But Xmas comes and the presents we get
Mean the nasty weather we can soon forget.

Spring brings hope of nicer days
The flowers bloom, look pretty and gay
The clocks go forward, more time for fun
We all start to enjoy the warming sun.

The seasons all offer different things
Some even make the birds sing
But altogether they make up one whole year
We know it, those of us that are here.

Matthew Chatfield (11)
Hasland Hall Community School

My Family

My family are the best
Even though my sister is a pest.

I have a mum and dad
Sometimes I think they are mad.

Sometimes my bedroom gets in a mess
Today my sister rescued a bird from a nest.

My best friend is called Ben
We have built a den.

We have got two dogs
They like to chew on logs.

My cat is called Pat
And it is very fat.

At work my dad drives a van
He is a very big man.

My mum cooks and cleans
She likes chicken nuggets and beans.

My grandma likes to feed the birds
She bakes cakes with lemon curd.

When I get home from school,
I like to go on the computer,
My dad tells me to get off my arse
And get on my scooter.

Mitchell Steele   (11)
Hasland Hall Community School

Hide-And-Seek

I have a secret hiding place,
Behind the garden shed.
No one thinks to look there,
So I'm on my own instead.

Jamie's hiding up a tree,
Hanging like a monkey.
Julie's stood behind the door,
Her clothes are really funky.

Nobody has found me yet,
They think that I'm next door.
Everyone's surrounding Jamie,
As he's fainted on the floor.

But I don't move a muscle,
I stay really still instead.
No one has found me yet,
Behind the garden shed.

I am really tired now,
It's getting time for bed.
But no one yet has found me,
And I haven't yet been fed.

My stomach is an empty pit,
My mouth is as dry as a desert,
I have to stand up, quiet and still,
It's really quite unpleasant.

No one ever finds me,
In my secret hiding place.
It would help if someone was playing with me,
But I'm too much of a disgrace.

Hannah Cullumbine (12)
Hasland Hall Community School

Changes

As I walk down the road
I see the leaves up in the trees,
Autumn gives them the colour of gold,
That's the sign they are getting old.

Winter will soon be here,
It will be cold with frosty snow,
Children will be playing snowballs,
Their faces will be aglow.

The bushes full of berries,
The branches full of snow,
It won't be long for spring again
Till the daffodils begin to show.

But come spring what will be seen,
The leaves on the trees
Will have turned a lovely new green.

Then along comes the summer,
Gardens and parks full of colour.
People like to walk in the parks
And see the lovely flowers,
I go in the park
And play with my friends for hours.

Ryan Higginbottom (12)
Hasland Hall Community School

Dad

Dad, always there for me.
Kind, devoted and strong,
Like a rock that will not move,
Like a shelter keeping me safe.
He makes me feel really happy,
Like Christmas Day.
Dad, makes me wish to be like him.

Martin Basford (12)
Hasland Hall Community School

Lunch Time In The Jungle

It's 1 o'clock and off goes the bell.
'It's lunch!' the wild animals yell.
They knock down the classroom door,
Crush their teacher to the floor.

They're louder than a jumbo jet,
And sure to make the teacher sweat.
They stampede, they thrash,
They're sure to give their teacher a rash.

The hungry hordes hurry,
They're hot and bothered, in a flurry,
They chomp, they gorge, they stuff their face,
But they're not in the Great North Race.

The teachers now take a break,
For their life's only sake.
A cup of tea, a piece of cake,
2 o'clock, a time teachers hate.

There is a substance that kids chew,
The table is what they stick it to.
It shouldn't end up in your tum,
It's supposedly called bubblegum.

So now you know about the jungle,
Next time your stomach makes a rumble,
Think about lunch at this school,
Where animals that are kids rule.

Oliver Hooper (12)
Hasland Hall Community School

The World

When it began, the world was a good space,
Gardens and green things were all over the place.
Lush meadows, country and plants,
All was as it should be, no war or violence.

Then came the Romans, with fighting and plunder,
For the peace of the world it was a serious blunder.

William the Conqueror, from France he came,
By his savage army, no one forgot his name.

Richard and Henry in a terrible mess,
But the Battle of Bosworth, for Richard, was death.

1900 was such a year for fighting,
Everyone against each other,
Seemed to be the general understanding.

WW1, such a gory battle,
Not many survived, not humans, nor cattle.

By 1935, the Nazis arrived,
But the book burning and their racism
Meant they were soon despised.

WW2, it went on for years.
For the allied forces, victory seemed far.

But then the great powers, led with such strength,
Ended it firmly, after such great length.

Saddam Hussein was hated by all,
Another war started, which only held trouble.

Robert Longstaff (12)
Hasland Hall Community School

Spring

Blossom on the trees,
Pink, orange and white.
A carpet of bluebells
Which look so bright.
Dandelions and daisies
Amongst the green,
Just waiting to be looked at,
Just waiting to be seen.
Leaves on the trees,
Flowers on the grass,
All signs of spring
As I walk past.
All signs of spring,
So let us sing
The beauty of nature,
It's finally spring.

Claire Storer (15)
Hasland Hall Community School

The Teacher-In-Training

The teacher-in-training is not very nice,
In fact I heard that he gave someone lice!
The teacher-in-training is horrid and cruel,
I heard that he called someone a mule!
The teacher-in-training isn't often awake,
I heard that he got bitten by a snake!
The teacher-in-training has a weird hair-do,
I heard from a friend that he is cuckoo!
The teacher-in-training deserves a mention,
I heard that (for nothing), he gave a detention!
The teacher-in-training has two pet mice,
And I say that he is actually nice!

Miranda King (12)
Hasland Hall Community School

When I Die, Don't Cry

Please don't cry
When I die,
For I have gone to a better place.
Far beyond the Earth and space.
So I can go and rest alone,
For this will be my new home.
I know someday we will meet again
And the love in our hearts will stay the same,
For I cannot love you more,
That's the only thing I know for sure.
Until that splendid day is here,
I want you to know I'll always be near.
I will be watching over you day and night,
All the time enjoying each sight.
You can't hear me, you can't see me,
Right from the start,
But every day I'll be in your heart.
So please don't cry
When I die.

Natalie Richards (12)
Hasland Hall Community School

Hopes And Dreams

My life's unfair, it's very mean,
That's why the television watching
Has got me chasing hopes and dreams.
Living a teenager's paradise
Shows you what life's really like.
Lying in hospital, looking at myself,
Realising that Heaven's not true
And that I'm going to Hell.
Looking at my life, I haven't been clever,
But looking at me 'n' Hollie, we're lasting forever.

Ben Elliott (15)
Hasland Hall Community School

Ascension

Glinting in the moon, a tongue of light illuminating the kitchen.
Fingers of death, sticking out above the wooden knife block.
Reach forwards,
Stretch towards them.

He doesn't love me,
He never will!
I will always love him.

Nobody loves me!

Just want it to be over.
No more of him laughing at me, teasing me.
No more!

No one will notice.
No one will miss me.
No one will care.

Holding the knife in shaking hands,
Tears drip down distraught cheeks.
Plunge it into soft flesh.
Blood soaks through onto clothes, forms a puddle on the floor.
Red reflection on the wooden door.

No more!

The church bell tolls sixteen times.
Once for each year of my life.

Charlotte Wilkins (16)
Hasland Hall Community School

Death

Death is something that happens to all,
It's an everlasting thing.
We all know that we'll die one day,
However much we sin,
But then which way will we go?
Towards the light, or towards the flames?
People we once knew or have yet to meet
Will be stood there calling our names.
It's not too late to change our lives,
To stop what we are doing wrong,
To change our direction for life after death,
Before we're dead and gone.

But when I'm gone, don't be sad,
Remember the happy times we had.

I know that I will die one day,
Don't mourn for me when I'm gone.
I'll be in a better place.
Live your life, move on.
Rejoice for all the days we spent
Together, happy and well,
Just think of where I'll go when I'm gone,
Paradise, not Hell.
Sing for me a happy song
The whole wide world can hear,
A song we'll remember together,
Never shed a tear.
We'll be reunited one day,
That I'm certain of,
For we have a bond so strong,
One of everlasting love.

Kearah Baker (14)
Hasland Hall Community School

Mrs Autumn

I heard Mrs Autumn coming,
She stretched her beautiful body.
Her nails shone brightly,
Like a light in the sky.

She whispered, 'I'll defrost the keyhole.
I'll sneak in your house,
I'll make your fires burn,
I'll light up the sky
So you can see,
And make every animal
As happy as can be.

Oh yes!
How you will smile and laugh,
And to make it more special,
I'll give you
Hallowe'en and bonfire night.'

Selena Clark (11)
Hasland Hall Community School

My Little Sister

My little sister's got the loudest scream in our school,
she loves *screaming* . . .

When she falls over in the playground and hurts herself,
you can hear her *screaming* . . .

Five whole streets away, no one except me can
get her to stop *screaming* . . .

Once she's started, my dad says it is like a riot.
So while she's *screaming* . . .

A teacher comes and fetches me and
I have to try and stop her *screaming* . . .

I love my little sister. I wish sometimes she was quite . . .

Glynn Allerton (11)
Hasland Hall Community School

Chesterfield FC

C is for chanting coming from the Kop
H is for home games we usually win
E is for enjoying watching them play
S is for sorrow watching them lose
T is for trophy, not many we've won
E is for Evatt scoring a goal!
R is for result, we hope it's a win
F is for field mouse, our famous mascot
I is for Innes getting sent off!
E is for everyone who unites when they play
L is for league, they are in league one
D is for defence, keeping out the goals

F is for floodlights to play in the dark
C is for Chesterfield, the best team of all!

Wayne Dove (12)
Hasland Hall Community School

Holiday In Gozo

H appy days
O n the beach
L ots of sun
I n the sky
D iving into the sea
A nd the water is so clear
Y ou can see the fish swimming underwater

I n the night
N ot a sound to disturb your silent slumber

G oing home
O n the way to catch a ferry
Z ooming along the winding roads
O h no! I've left my purse back at the hotel!

Amy Birch (12)
Hasland Hall Community School

Excuse Me Waiter

Excuse me Waiter, if you please,
There's something weird inside the cheese.
I ate a piece, it made me sneeze,
Excuse me Waiter, if you please.

Excuse me Madam, may I say,
I never touched it anyway.
Today just must not be your day,
Excuse me Madam, may I say.

Excuse me Waiter, if you please,
There's a funny taste within the peas.
It feels like I've been stung by bees,
Excuse me Waiter, if you please.

Excuse me Madam, that's untrue,
This food wasn't just made for you.
Wait a sec, there's another batch due,
Excuse me Madam, that's untrue.

Rebecca Turner (12)
Hasland Hall Community School

Shopping

From shorts to trousers to jeans to skirts,
From vest tops to T-shirts to halter-necks and shirts,
From shoes, jewellery and bags,
And all my favourite teen mags,
I like to shop and shop and shop and shop.
I like to shop till I drop.

From labels to nice clothes and diamond rings,
And all the rest of my favourite things,
From New Look to Kookai and Top Shop,
Where I think I'll buy a new top.
I like to shop and shop and shop and shop,
I like to shop till I drop.

Louisa Hartley (13)
Hasland Hall Community School

The Haunted House

In the haunted house,
With the haunted kitchen,
Best get out quick,
Or you'll start itchin'
For the ghosts in the house
Don't like visitors, not even a mouse.

Please be careful,
Please beware,
Please enter
If you dare.

In the haunted house
With the haunted loft,
The ghosts in there
Make you go soft.
For the ghosts go bang
And the ghouls go boom,
They fill the air
With a feel of *doom!*

Please be careful,
Please beware,
Please enter
If you dare.

Katie Ogden (12)
Hasland Hall Community School

Playing In The Park

It took a lot of force
to move the bouncing rocking-horse.
Then as I went to glide,
I fell down the slippery slide.
Then I saw what looked like a funnel,
it was only a big, dark tunnel.
Then I fell into a trench,
trying to get to a broken bench.

So I decided to have a swing
on the famous rocking swing.
While thinking of the Popstars UK Tour,
me and my friend were on the swaying see-saw.
It was too late and turning dark
while I was playing in the park,
So I had to leave straight away,
to go back another day.

Rebecca Tye (12)
Hasland Hall Community School

My Rabbit

I have a rabbit
She is called Bella,
She lives in a hutch.
She has straw for a bed.
She eats food,
She likes broccoli and apples best.
She goes in her run
Which is on the lawn.
Her favourite toy is a plant pot,
Which she likes to throw around.
She likes to nibble the grass,
She is very friendly
And likes to be stroked.
She is very nosy,
And likes to know what you are doing.

Edward Brooks (12)
Hasland Hall Community School

Our Street

In our family there are five,
But only me mam and dad can drive.
It's a good job, cos we're never in,
Us kids we do everything.

'Er next door, she's 'avin' a baby,
If it's a girl she'll call it Sadie.
If it's a boy, she doesn't know,
Either way it's gonna grow.

Over the road there live two lads,
One 'as a beard same 'as 'is dad's.
Trouble is he's only ten,
He shaves it off - it grows back again.

Some on our street think they're really posh,
They think they've got a lot of dosh,
But really they're as poor as us,
I've seen 'er mam get on the bus.

There is an old lady who lives on 'er own,
She bust 'er hip and crawled to the phone,
Ambulance came and took 'er away,
Me mam and dad said, 'I hope she's OK.'

A woman went missing four doors down,
She was last seen in London Town.
'Er husband didn't seem to care,
Cos a new woman moved in with blonde hair.

Some strange goings on in our street if you look,
Enough goings on you could write a book.
But for now my poem 'as come to an end,
Cos I'm goin' round corner to see me friend.

Abbie Johnson (12)
Hasland Hall Community School

The Natural World

There are many different types of trees,
Many insects like all the bees.
There are many creatures like tiny mice,
And lots of food like veg and rice.

There are all sorts of plants,
And other things like fish or ants.
There are beautiful birds
And cattle in herds.

There are many types of cats,
Then there are slightly smaller things, like rats.
There are many different dogs
And lots of little frogs.

There are lots of pretty feathers,
And different types of weather.
All the lovely flowers
Have great powers
To make this world so beautiful.

Emma Fowler (12)
Hasland Hall Community School

What A Load Of Rubbish

I like the world, but why do people spoil it?
The world is not a pit, where people throw rubbish in it.
I don't want unnecessary buildings,
This is when I get a funny feeling,
But in the end, will anyone care
When the world is bare?
I've thought of this for years,
But other people rather drink beers.
I think people are going crazy,
As they'd rather be lazy.
So when you next throw rubbish,
You might be the cause of the world to finish.

David Waddington (12)
Hasland Hall Community School

Summer's End

I walk into the warm fresh air
and gaze upon the flowers there.
The sun is shining on my face,
it really is a special place.
Underneath the bright blue sky
I hear the gentle breezes sigh.
Sweet-smelling grass beneath my feet,
the birds looking for worms to eat.
All too soon the sun grows low
and summer turns to winter snow.
Glistening frost on hedges bare,
where once there were flowers there.
The twittering birds no longer play,
they do not like the colder day.
Now the garden lays at rest,
a summer garden is really best.

Sarah Billyeald (13)
Hasland Hall Community School

Laugh

Laughter of adults, children and teens
Can be heard and seen.

Laughter is not a word with no meaning,
It expresses happiness and few other feelings.

Few people use laughing therapy!
To calm down when they are angry!
But most think that it's used when you're happy.

There is no cost for laughing
And there is no strict law for laughter,
So laugh, laugh and laugh.

Laugh in every season,
But don't laugh with any reason!
So, laugh and the world shall laugh with you!

Dania Qamar (12)
Hasland Hall Community School

Home At Last

The howling wind blew through the trees,
The freezing cold nipped at my toes.
The snow came right up past my knees,
The land was shaking to and fro.

I hurried through the woods so scared,
It was so dark, so cold, so still.
Didn't know what was lurking there,
I quickly ran towards the hill.

When I'd climbed to the very top,
No time to pause for a little rest,
My body was about to flop,
My heart was pounding in my chest.

I approached the house stood proudly,
It was shelter from the storm.
I heard his voice calling loudly,
Shouting, 'Come inside, get warm!'

No longer was I wet and cold,
But cosy, dry and feeling snug.
Glad to be back into the fold,
I fell asleep on the rug.

Ami Evans (13)
Hasland Hall Community School

Little Sisters

My little sister is called Rebecca,
She can be bossy, but I don't hate her.
When she's in a good mood, you will get a cuddle.
When she's in a bad mood, all you get is trouble.
Her room is full of Barbie dolls and cuddly toys,
Beware this girl's room is not for boys.
There you go, all I've got to say,
My little sister, she's OK.

Keri Winfield (12)
Hasland Hall Community School

The Match

I ran onto the pitch . . .
Number five printed on my back,
The other team approached like Vikings.
The whistle shrieked from the man in black.

We kicked off . . .
As the boy passed back to me,
I smacked the ball up front,
As far as I could see.

We were losing 3-0 at half-time,
The drinks were passed around,
Then we were ready for some action,
But the ref was nowhere to be found.

We couldn't find him anywhere,
We searched through hedges and all over land,
We didn't see him for ten minutes,
Then we found him with a Bovril in his hand.

He looked up to see me standing there,
He apologised and ran to the pitch.
My dad yelled, 'Come on ref.'
The ref said, 'I've got a terrible stitch.'

Finally the match was over, we lost 7-0,
Our manager was quite angry and mad,
As the ref went off to finish is Bovril.
I don't think I played too bad!

Daniel Wheeler (12)
Hasland Hall Community School

On Her Own

Love is a sign
Of freedom,
When people cry
And people laugh.

Look down into
Your heart
And see how happy
These two are.

All in white
And all in black,
Smiling, thinking
Of happy thoughts.
Loving each other.
Is it special or
Is it being
Kind and loyal?

Let her go on
Her own to be
With her love.
Just be quiet,
Not a word.
Let her go on
Her own to love
This man on
Her own.

Tessa Simon (13)
Hasland Hall Community School

Yet Another War

Yet another war.
The reason? Weapons of mass destruction in Iraq,
Or so they say.
Have we all conveniently forgotten Hiroshima?

The thought of war, biological and chemical weapons petrifies me,
Causes sleepless nights full of fear.
War was declared, my nightmare becomes reality,
Will this lead to more 9/11s?

Bloodshed, bombs, brutality, battle, Bush and Blair -
                                    create devastation.
They searched in vain - no weapons of mass destruction could
                                    be found.

Was this just an excuse for war?
Was the oozing of oil too tempting to resist?

Why the need to fight, I ask - why the need to murder the innocent,
Caught up in the struggle?
Louis Armstrong once sang, 'What A Wonderful World' - which world?
This one - that condones the wrongful killing of thousands?
Which allows people to live in daily fear for their lives?

All different, all equal - all deserve a chance.
Living together in constant terror.
Why fight - not talk? Why war - not peace?
The torture continues. War. Fear. Is there any hope for us?

Don't fight terrorists with terrorism.
Talk, make peace - show heroism.

Georgia Powell (15)
Hasland Hall Community School

My Favourite Friends

My favourite friends are my two dogs,
Billy and Bobby.
They're there for me whenever I'm down,
They're there when I wear a frown.

Furry Labradors are my ideal friends,
Sometimes they send you round the bend.
They are so soft and they are so cute,
They're much cuter than Jenna's pet newt.

I love them more than chocolate and sweets,
They are addicted to many meats.
Beef, lamb, pork and chicken,
And in their food bowl that's where the meat's sticking.

Training them is easy,
Playing with them is hard.
I will always love them anyway,
Because if I'm in trouble,
They are my little guards.

Hayley Levick (12)
Hasland Hall Community School

Ferrari

The Ferrari's red coat gleams in the sunlight,
Its wing mirrors glint as it turns right.
It proudly wears its badge of a prancing horse,
As it accelerates with such force.

As I put my pedal to the floor,
I hear its engine roar.
I wind my window down
As I go speeding through the town.

As the traffic lights turn red,
I apply the brakes and stop it dead.
As I open the scissor doors,
I stare down at the prancing horse.

Sean Mosley (13)
Hasland Hall Community School

Hallowe'en Horrors

I like Hallowe'en,
It makes some people scream.

With all those treats,
I love those sweets,
Crunchy, munchy,
I do like Hallowe'en.

All those costumes look brill,
If you make them yourself, it's a great skill.
Witches, devils, ghosts and more,
I do like Hallowe'en.

They all look very scary,
They're not fairies.
I do like Hallowe'en.

Natalie Fairbrother (12)
Hasland Hall Community School

At The Zoo

I saw the sea lions play with a ball,
Giraffes are tall,
Mice are small,
Lions maul,
Elephants call,
And the monkeys all climb up the wall,
Some of them fall.

For dinner we took sandwiches,
On them they had cheese, jam and ham.
We did not park very well, it was a tight squeeze.
On the way, there was a traffic jam.
Also for dinner, my brother had fish, chips and peas.

Lucy Bramley (12)
Hasland Hall Community School

A Mixed Up Hallowe'en

I know a mummy, he's a floaty sort of guy,
When he's out, he's a little shy,
He doesn't like spookin'
But he's always up for groovin'
That's a mixed up Hallowe'en.

A ghost is my mate,
He doesn't like to be late,
He looks evil and green,
But he's not that mean,
That's a mixed up Hallowe'en.

I've got a pumpkin,
Who likes to be filled with gin,
She flies on a broom,
And says Frankenstein's her groom,
That's a mixed up Hallowe'en!

A party's good, this time of year,
All the adults keep drinking beer,
They all get their chance,
Then see my dad dance,
That really is a mixed up Hallowe'en.

Lauren Winnard (12)
Hasland Hall Community School

Christmas

C hildren playing in the snow,
H e is singing 'Ho, ho, ho!'
R unning while the snow is setting,
 I n suspense of what they're getting.
S leeping quietly in their beds,
T ightly clutching their favourite teds.
'M erry Christmas everyone,
A ll the jobs are now done!
S o have a merry Christmas,
    ho, ho, ho till next time!'

Stephen Hockey (12)
Hasland Hall Community School

The Sheffield Mariner

Come all ye jolly seamen bold,
And listen unto me,
And I to you will a tale unfold
Of the dangers of the sea.

Of shipwrecks and disasters,
That unto me befell,
When I sailed from Sheffield to Rotherham
On the Sheffield ship canal.

The captain was a nobleman's son,
Who came from West Bar green,
Where he kept a large establishment
Selling Hokey-Pokey ice cream.

The first mate was an Irishman,
They called him Paddy Doyle,
And all the water he gave to us
Was a can of paraffin oil.

We sailed away from Sheffield
On a snowy summer's day,
Five and twenty dumb men
Shouted, 'Hip, hip, hooray.'

We arrived at the port of Attacliff,
Where they live on shavings and muck,
And after we sailed away from there,
We had some terrible luck.

We no but got to Coleridge Road,
We ran upon a whale,
To save the ship from getting wet,
We hung it on a nail.

When we got to Templeborough,
A pirate hove in sight,
And all the crew began to sing,
'Oh we don't want to fight.'

When we got to Rotherham,
We ran upon some rocks,
But we were rescued by the
Lifeboat launch cat that came from Tinsley docks.

The ship is now in a pawnshop,
The crew in Wakefield jail,
And I'm the only liar left
To tell this terrible tale.

Christopher Jackson (13)
Hasland Hall Community School

Dragsters

They roar down the track
like dragons with fire
and clouds of black smoke.
Their hearts are made of iron,
their bodies in a bright metal cloak,
they flash past the crowds, screaming.
The glory is theirs for the taking,
the dragons who race on the circuit,
only the records to break.

Samuel Heywood (12)
Hasland Hall Community School

Sadness

Sadness is a plant that grows in the soil,
It wraps round your mind and pricks your brain,
Love turns to hate,
Happy to sad,
It takes control and makes you mad.
You fill with rage,
Trapped in a cage,
You just let it out,
Scream and shout.

Karl Dodds (12)
Hasland Hall Community School

Friends

I have special friends
Who can tell me the latest fashion trends.
Someone I can tell secrets to,
Someone I can show stuff that's new.

They are always there for me,
They are there when I scrape my knee.
We are a very happy little group,
Altogether our brains are a bad loop-de-loop!

They act like silly little monkeys,
But some of them are punkies.
They're a right horrible lot,
So whatever you do, forget them not!

Zoë Turner (12)
Hasland Hall Community School

My Holidays

I love going on holiday, do you want to know why?
Because on the way there, you watch the world go by.

The best bit is packing because you don't know what to take,
You need clothes, stuff, something for the way, even just for one day.

I also love camping, sitting round the fire.

Eating sweets, having treats,
And when it becomes night,
It's black and dark,
But I like it that way.

Danielle Kirk (12)
Hasland Hall Community School

Disappear

Some say that she was lonely,
Some say she was not all there,
But the truth of her life was worse,
As she wandered in despair.

No one lived to comfort her,
Inside she felt shut out,
As if closed in a hall of glass,
Trying hard to burst out.

She always dreamed of freedom,
Her eyes would fill with tears,
As much she hoped, much she wished,
To fade and disappear.

At last she obtained freedom,
Like a puppet detached from her strings,
Having finally disappeared,
She felt she had grown wings.

It happened on a starry night,
When street lamps brightly shone,
She woke up very suddenly
And found that she was gone.

Rowena Lord (12)
Hasland Hall Community School

Cape Horn

Thunder rolls across the skies,
Lightning flashes like devil's eyes,
Waves toss, their fathoms deep,
Down they plunge and up they leap.

Sinisterly the clouds loom,
Threatening to present their doom,
Rain thrashes like a whip,
Quickly covering the ship.

'Furl the sails, the winds are high,'
So up the sailors climb to try,
As the captain bellows,
They fight elemental foes.

Like the ice upon the ropes,
Frozen are the sailors' hopes,
They doubt they'll beat the storm,
That has claimed lives at Cape Horn.

They fight the merciless seas,
Then the eye of the storm reprieves,
They've defeated death's way,
For before them is a bay!

Any port in a storm!

Holly Bee (11)
Hope Valley College

Anthony Horowitz

A glinting gun upon a chair,
A shining knife in a teddy bear,
A sly black cat in the dead of night,
Plotting to fight a fight,
A cup of poison in his belt,
The big red sun begins to melt.

A fast red car goes streaming past,
With loud, loud music making a blast,
The car goes down a secret alley,
And shoots a lady practising ballet,
The rain falls down but is still sunny,
The car still goes to make more money.

A secret book dripped in blood,
The car drives through a load of mud,
To a place where drugs are sold,
To people who are young and old,
A man breathes his last breath,
As he faces his death.

Jack Hardwick (11)
Lady Manners School

Warrior

A gleaming sword flashed through the air,
As it cut down the form of his enemy,
His powerful stallion sped through the woods,
To flee the scene of the crime,
The wood broke and he came to knoll,
Over that hill, 'A foe!' he cried,
His strong hand strung the cord on bow,
The cord relaxed as the arrow whistled along,
It soared into the neck of the outlaw,
Relief rushed through his bold heart.

Joe Shallow (11)
Lady Manners School

Deep In The Dark Cave

Going past trees
Going past trees,
You feel the breeze,
I am doing something,
What am I doing?

Deep in the dark cave,
Deep in the dark cave,
You can see nothing,
You need a really bright torch,
So you can see where you are going.

All about bats
All about bats,
You can see cats,
But in the dark you can see the cat's eyes.

Keeley Jarvis (11)
Lady Manners School

My Mum

A lady sits with a cup of steaming hot tea in her hands,
She lies back onto the blue leather sofa,
And carefully places the cup on the floor,
Then she picks up a murder novel from next to her and starts to read,
A beam of sunlight floods the room,
Illuminating the pale white rose that sits on the mantelpiece,
Hours pass,
But she's still there,
And then as silently as a mouse,
She falls into a dreamless sleep.

Helena Dawson (12)
Lady Manners School

School

What is the point of homework?
I really don't have a clue,
We do enough work at school,
And then have to work at home too.

I mean it's child labour!
Teachers should be put behind bars,
And they're all so weird, teachers, I mean,
Maybe they all come from Mars.

They think that there's not enough school,
And not enough time to subtract,
They're all mad I tell you,
But one day, I'll get my own back!

Rebecca James (11)
Lady Manners School

Sir Lancelot

In the woods with knights that say 'Ni,'
If you look, you will see,
The rather odd castle of Camelot,
A bold, old knight of Lancelot.

People like him there are few,
Shining helmet, eyes bright blue,
He has fought a killer bunny rabbit from the killing brigade,
Armed with only a holy hand grenade.

But in the end he was arrested,
For cutting off a famous historian's head.

Henry Jepson (11)
Lady Manners School

An Autumn Walk

The leaves, red, yellow, brown and gold fall gracefully
To the ground, leaving the trees to shiver with cold.
As I walk by, I pull my scarf up close to my neck
And my hat over my ears,
I notice strange fungi and mushrooms growing,
And then as I am looking at them
I notice that some are in a ring shape.
A fairy ring,
But I carry on, knowing that fairies are watching me,
I see a robin chirping away merrily to himself,
On a nearby holly bush, he seems to be smiling at me,
So I smile back.
I begin to enter the village, I see people I know,
I am so very cold,
Finally I reach my house, and now I am going to make myself
Some hot chocolate and warm myself by the blazing fire.

Sophie Townsend (11)
Lady Manners School

Queen Elizabeth

She would be sitting in the beautiful palace ballroom,
Watching the graceful snowflakes fall,
Drinking a sparkling glass of champagne,
Tomorrow she would be sitting in the back of a golden
                                    horse pulled carriage
Watching all of London whiz past;
She would come back to the palace,
And walk gracefully round the gardens sniffing the rich red roses,
At the end of the day she would sit on her throne,
Listening to her favourite violin classical music.

Ashleigh McMahon (11)
Lady Manners School

Avatar Of Elf Dale

(Avatar Min is a character from the book I am writing - 'Elf Dale')

Avatar Min wanders through the forest,
His movements graceful like a warrior,
He himself is like a deadly weapon that dances the dance
Of death in a hand of a soldier.

He sits by the bank of the stream gazing upon its beauty,
His eyes pass over the stream, no longer cool and refreshing,
It was hot and sticky tainted with evil magic and blood.

He is now rejected by all who know who he is,
Yet still he wanders slowly like a sorrowful song
                                    played on a lone violin,
He never has time to enjoy life,
For everything important to him is gone.

He tries to help but is always rejected,
He never quits he is like a strong powerful horse
Riding into a harsh wind.
He is a lone elf, yet his ideals carry him on.

Though scruffy in looks, he is like a glass of
Good red wine, regal yet wild.
He is powerful and graceful like a dark sky
With a storm brewing.

He fights for justice and his long dead race,
For he longs for the days of old when he could sit with
His family and friends and live his life.

He is Avatar Min.

Corey Christian (12)
Lady Manners School

Time For Scary School

Walking down the corridor,
Shouting, swearing,
Laughing, glaring.

School as big as the universe,
Confusing, huge, lost.

Sitting in the classroom,
Scribble, drone,
Boring, moan.

Scary as a monster,
Big kids,
Cramped, no friends.

Trying to get lunch,
Pushing, shoving,
Chewing, munching.

Oh no,
I forgot,
I can't remember,
I'm lost,
I don't understand,
School's so different and new.

Rules, more rules,
Terrifying teachers,
A dark, dark cave,
Time for scary school.

Lauren Hughes (11)
Landau Forte College

Life Seems Hard

Long days ahead
Seven sessions a day
(Way too many)
Life seems hard.

Lockers at the floor,
Feet trampling over work
(In very narrow corridors)
Life seems hard.

Lots of students
Many tall
(Compared with Year 7s)
Life seems hard.

Lots and lots of homework,
Not enough time to do it,
(Books piling up)
Life seems hard.

Finally it's time to go,
Suddenly forgotten everything
(Smiles upon your face)
Life is good.

Christopher Griffiths (11)
Landau Forte College

Remember Me

As you look at the poppy grown field,
Remember me,
Waiting for the end,
Remember me,
Abandoning the Earth,
Remember me,
This is the end,
Remember me.

Stacey Hyndman (13)
Landau Forte College

School Memories

Million voices, million people,
Corridors cramped, 10 deep queues,
Have to wait,
Don't want to,
I'm in an everlasting queue,
Moving an inch every hour or two.

Toilets are salons, well, the girls,
Hairbrushes, mascara, eyeliner, perfume,
Sweet smells.

Everything organised,
Times, lessons, rooms, tutors,
Just as organised as a lawyer,
We'd win a prize.

People really nice, good point,
I like this school really,
Maybe I exaggerated a little bit,
But only a little bit.
Really!

Monique Foster (11)
Landau Forte College

School Poem

One bright, sunny day of school,
The first day of school,
The school's huge, the classroom is *big*,
I'm big, I'm all grown up,
I love my new school,
It's cool!

Melissa Archer (11)
Landau Forte College

Massive

Pushing people in the corridors,
Hungry people in the canteen,
Nice people helping me out,
Everyone's in this massive cave.

The queues for the vending machines are stressful,
As the older kids push you around,
The corridors are so mind-boggling,
You're scared of being late,
Locker keys break, swipe cards are lost
Is anything at all simple?

Towering people on the tennis courts,
Older people in my tutor group,
Kind people show me the way,
Everyone's in this massive cave.

The phone continuously ringing and disturbing,
As the teacher hands out bad notes,
The stairs are so confusing,
You're scared of tripping down,
Ties are twisted, blazers are ripped,
Is anything at all simple?

Nervous people in my class,
Big kids in the corridors,
Scary teachers around every corner,
Everyone's in this massive cave.

Emily Watson (11)
Landau Forte College

When She Left

I still remember when she left me,
On that dark winter's night.
I told her to wrap up warm,
But that would not help,
Her skin went so cold,
It felt like ice running down my spine.

When I found her again, she was sleeping,
Sleeping in the darkness of the alley,
I looked at her, withering, decaying, failing,
She looked so peaceful,
But she was lifeless and pale.

As she was moved to her wooden bed,
And taken to a place where everyone slept,
Amongst the headstones,
Her memory burned in my head.

Andrew Dean (13)
Landau Forte College

Loneliness

Every day drags on when you're not there,
Memories lost that leave me in pieces,
The depressing sound of silence,
Leaves me sat there shattered.

I feel isolated when you're not there,
My injured heart hits the ground,
When I think about you it's gone,
I feel friendless and lonely.

Hannah Cooper (13)
Landau Forte College

What Graceful Pose

What graceful pose does the soldier have,
Scattering the ashes in a crimson sea,
The cold memorial of the withering fire,
Weeping for the ones we've lost.

What gory sight would sober,
The drunkest of us all,
My heart decayed as I saw her,
Touching my remnants.

Why did it take me away from her?
Piercing my core,
The bullet that came to my heart
Made me lose my love.

The world is obsolete,
Burning with the flame of passion,
In the war of irony.

Paris Sullivan (13)
Landau Forte College

School Poem

Frightened as a mouse,
Wanted to stay in my house,
That is my first day at school.

'I feel sick from my Mc Turk,'
I don't really want to work,
That is what I said.

Help! Help! I'm lost,
Stuck out here in the frost,
I don't want to go.

Matthew Swain (11)
Landau Forte College

Injured Heart

The burning sun is setting,
And my withering heart is
Sinking into its fiery depths.
The torment I feel is like
A disease killing my soul.

My loved one has departed,
And taken my shattered heart with her,
I remember a time
When the songbirds sang
Their sorrowful tune
And an envelope of anguish,
Graced my doorstep.

I cannot fight my injured heart,
I cannot heal the wound.

Sophie Porter (13)
Landau Forte College

Gone

Lifeless memories, no comfort now,
My love has departed,
But his spirit's still with me,
His body gone to never return.

My sorrow and anguish,
With my suffering heartache,
I need to put an end to my misery
And grief before I decay into nothing.

Abandoned and no sense of hope,
I will die a brutal death,
Only to know no one will
Be devastated,
No one to care.

Michelle Hill (13)
Landau Forte College

School Memories

The rushing corridors,
People going for their break,
Students talking, students chatting,
Students trapped in a classroom like a prison cell,
You'd better not dwell in the toilets, you may get caught.

Voices shouting, students banging like mad gorillas,
Strange new faces, tying up laces,
Then the corridors are quiet,
It will start again,
A new lesson begins.

People singing in the music room,
From the science labs you can hear a boom,
When you are in drama,
You could wish you were a carver,
When you are in dance,
You feel like you're doing a prance,
When you are in maths,
You sometimes feel that you want a bath.

Geography works with maps,
Sometimes you can do laps in PE,
The restaurant makes you want to eat,
The staff recommend you have a seat.

So now you've heard about my first few weeks,
Some of these you might seek.

Olivia Smith (11)
Landau Forte College

Mournful Losses

Of all these withering poppies here,
On the outskirts of an oblique, obliterated France,
There is one hopeful, gracious plant full of my love,
The love, for my lost one,
That I lost years ago.

His body now decaying,
In his cold dark grave,
I sob, my heart now broken,
Just think he was chucked in a dirty pit, not caring for his name.
I stand here today not knowing where he is,
No record, no headstone of where his body now lies.

Rest in peace my darling Tom,
I will never forget,
Those loving days we used to have,
When we were just lovesick teenagers.

Now I must go, far, far away,
But I will take this flower to remember you by,
As this is the only thing I have of yours.
Apart from those loving letters you sent me long ago,
Those words will always be in my heart,
But soon this flower will wilt and die,
Just like I am inside right now.

Ben Wilton (13)
Landau Forte College

Insecure

To be thrown from an injured love,
Is in some eyes a joyous occasion,
Not for me,
Such a tragedy is this sorrowful bereavement,
That the previously shining flower inside me,
Now wilts and withers without an ounce of hope to cling on to,
My distressed life is without a life,
Lifeless, sustaining a state of a shattered mirror,
Bad luck for life, that's me.

She has left now,
Walked out of my life,
No disturbance, no letter,
No conflict,
I hate it,
I search for a reason within myself,
Pondering on whether another man is in the picture,
I'm sure of it now,
Demoted to the free cash injection,
Ran off with my wages.

Now, I'm not sure how I can trust anyone,
Myself.

Chris Thomas (13)
Landau Forte College

When I Started School

When I started school I was really scared,
When I started school I was ready and prepared,
When I started school I dropped my books,
Because I was worried about my looks.
When I started school I had to catch the bus,
When I started school I made such a fuss,
When I started school I was really tired,
When I started school I was scared I was going to be fired.

Kate Patterson (11)
Landau Forte College

School Life

Queues, a long 50-foot python, seeming to last for miles,
Corridors, a swarming beehive of people,
Piles and piles,
Lessons are boring, fading away,
Teachers are many,
Saying what they have to say.
Horrific noise; shattering ears,
Extra long day, seeming to last for years,
Strange new faces staring down at you,
Homework stacked up like the Eiffel Tower,
So much to do.
Fierce tutors are bloodthirsty bulls,
Raring to be set free,
Friendly tutors are loving puppies, wagging their tails at me.

School life goes on good or bad,
All the lessons we have had,
We learn new things every day,
School's difficult, that's what I'd say!

Daniel Bown (11)
Landau Forte College

Old School

Old friends,
3 head teachers,
1 classroom,
Very small,
Good times,
Bad times,
Best friend goes,
Still know him,
Christmas parties,
And productions,
That's how it goes.

Jack Smith (11)
Landau Forte College

My Friend Joe

All day, all I think,
Is about my friend Joe.
Every time I talk, think or blink,
I remember the killing by the foe.

How could he depart and leave me,
Straight in the chest, he was shot.
As I was hiding behind a tree,
How cruelly he left me and pushed off.

How sudden evil unleashed!
As soon as he went,
So brave he must have been,
Now I'm stranded in Kent.

Joe will always remain in my mind,
And I have to move on,
But I can't leave Joe behind,
He was my friend, not a con!

Gurveer Singh Hansi (14)
Landau Forte College

There's No Hope!

The accent I speak,
Makes me feel abnormal,
I feel as if I am a different species,
As I think of my future,
There's no hope!

Why do they think I am so different,
Just because I come from London?
I don't speak a different language!
Hopefully this will pass,
But I don't see any hope,
With being able to fit in.

Hannah Nichols-Green (12)
Landau Forte College

Alone

I stood there alone,
The wind pushing me,
I stared at them,
They stared at me.

I felt alone,
Though children were all around me,
All in their own little groups.

I prayed and prayed that I could
Just fade away,
But I was left standing there alone.

I missed my friends,
I missed my teachers,
I missed being happy,
I didn't want to be alone.

Silpa Gembali (12)
Landau Forte College

I Moved From London

I moved from London,
And what do I see?
A brand new life
Staring at me.

I moved from London,
And what do I feel?
A scared sensation,
Beginning to unpeal.

I moved from London,
And what do I hear?
My heavy breathing,
I try to hide my fear.

Sarah Allsopp (13)
Landau Forte College

First Day At School

It's my first day of school,
Make new friends while on the bus,
Proud parents making a fuss.

Get in the building,
Big, new, open spaces,
New faces.

Strict new dress code,
Must get to lessons on time,
Being late is a crime.

Get my books,
Pens and pencils everywhere,
Harsh new teachers are a scare.

The day is over,
I want to stay,
Can't wait to come back the next day.

Laura Maskrey (12)
Landau Forte College

Let Me Have It Back!

Come here,
My tears are thundering down,
I need help,
They cost so many pounds.

I need it well,
Not down,
Just let it be,
Please,
Please,
Please.

Tamika Short (12)
Landau Forte College

SATs

SATs, SATs, SATs,
Science, English, maths,
Level 5, 4 or 3,
Why are these subjects bothering me?
Why do these numbers seem so high?
This is one of those days when you want to skive,
Dip, dodge, dive,
These 3 things taking up my time!
SATs, SATs, SATs,
Now we're all playing with rounders' bats,
SATs are over now!
I wonder how I did - I wonder how?
Results are back!
At last!
3 - 4 - 5?
This is one of those days when you want to skive.

Ann-Marie Hitchcock (12)
Landau Forte College

Bullying

Everywhere I look to the left, to the right,
Sad faces, I know they couldn't sleep at night!

Bullying is not nice, it makes people sad,
I can't understand why they do it, it makes me so mad.

That kind of behaviour makes me shudder,
Let's all get on with life and be nice to each other.

Let's all be grateful that we are alive, healthy not sad,
This life is too short, to treat others so bad.

Sam Gandy (12)
Landau Forte College

Learning Jungle

A school is like a jungle,
Bursting with noise from top to bottom,
Filled with kids like jungle animals,
Where we have to hunt every day.

In my learning jungle,
There are kids of different races,
Like they have been thrown up in the air,
And caught muddled up.

In my learning jungle,
We learn to make resources,
And learn to feed ourselves,
For a long time to come.

In my learning jungle now,
We are learning new languages,
So we can talk to people far away,
Now my learning jungle,
Is here to stay.

Jordan Britton (11)
Landau Forte College

Will They Laugh At Me?

In a new school, far from home,
Everyone seems so relaxed,
Will they laugh at me?
I feel such a fool,
Why did Mum and Dad make me come here?
Will I have any friends
Or will they all pick on me?
I feel such a fool,
My accent may be different,
But surely they won't mind?

Navdeep Kaur Johal (12)
Landau Forte College

Memories

Another day has gone, memories passing by,
The first day I went to school, I began to cry.

But I got over it and made a few friends,
In school I've been through some sharp turns and bends.

But I've tried hard and I can't do more than that,
On Red Nose Day, my teacher wore a silly hat.

In school, I've always done as I was told,
I mean, come on, I'm as good as gold.

Only joking, I'm really a little devil,
Even though in SATs, I got quite a high level.

Yeah, they were the good times
Messing around in my old school,
The teachers couldn't keep up,
They always thought they were cool.

But everyone is moving on,
The teachers are moving on,
My friends are moving on,
Into the big wide world.

Charlton Kent (12)
Landau Forte College

Cool School!

Secondary school,
It's so cool,
Very nervous,
Teachers strict,
Have to be quick,
Tick, tock, tick,
Hometime at last!

Kathryn Loveless (11)
Landau Forte College

My Nightmare Of School

I ran to the door,
Excited beyond reason,
Sadly the noise hit me,
Like a mad lion roar.

I ran left and right,
Frightened and lost,
I ran into a boy,
And I was in a fight.

The punches hit me in the mouth and face,
I turned tail and ran,
Not looking and by accident,
I tripped over a briefcase.

Blood on my jacket and on my shirt,
I ran up the stairs and
Ran to the nurse,
She told me to go outside,
And I fell into the dirt.
All of this happened in my
Nightmare of school.

Ryan Joyce (11)
Landau Forte College

Another Day At School

Another day at school, my friend's always there,
The hall always full, another day at school,
As I line up for dinner, the queue is so long,
I will be waiting all day, another day at school,
It is the end of the day,
Soon to be another day at school.

Gareth Povey (11)
Landau Forte College

School Seasons Poem!

In the winter days of school,
The wind whistles through the glass window,
Cold and scared,
Tortures of slow starvation's,
All there is a long sigh of sorrow.

In the spring days of school,
Starting to get warmer,
The sun peaks through the clouds,
With a glinting sign of the sunset.

In the summer days of school,
Hot! Hot! Hot!
Sweaty and tired,
But you definitely feel more energetic.

In the autumn days of school,
Leaves on trees fall and trickle,
All crimpled and scarlet,
Like whirlwinds spinning round non stop.

Parveen Kaur Thandi (11)
Landau Forte College

Landau Forte College

I don't like some lessons,
I do like some lessons,
At the start of school I am ready to go,
At the end of school I am very slow,
Lessons are never-ending,
Days are longer than ever.

Timothy Riley (11)
Landau Forte College

My First Day Of School!

My first day of secondary school was quite scary,
The lessons, they all vary,
When I walked through that theatre door,
I got one piece of homework, then more,
And I thought, *oh maybe I'll faint,*
I never know, maybe we'll paint,
Every day I get home, I feel so tired,
But now I'm in school, it feels like I've been hired,
I really thought I wouldn't fit in,
I kind of feel like a falling pin,
Only because of the amount of homework I get,
I'm feeling that maybe I'll get the hang of things, I bet,
But on the other hand, school is cool,
And I hope I never break the rules!

Elicia Redfern (11)
Landau Forte College

First Day At School

Nervous, nervous,
Taking deep breathes,
Waiting patiently,
Looking around,
Gradually people liking me,
Going outside,
Playing football, everyone likes me,
Going outside,
I see my mate in Year B,
He takes me around,
And the first day is over - whoo!
But now I'm used to it,
And everyone likes me.

Taraseen Iqbal (11)
Landau Forte College

School! School! School!

When I started school, it was really scary,
When I started school, I was very wary,
I had to carry heavy books,
I remember getting unusual looks.

At dinner we had lots of tasty food,
And we're not allowed to be rude,
Some people did not talk to others,
Some of my friends had older brothers.

We could learn lots of new things in maths,
In geography we would be following footpaths,
I would sometimes watch the birds,
And in English learn new words.

At 3.45 we would go home,
And have to do my homework all alone.

Kelly-Ann Hutchinson (11)
Landau Forte College

School Day

The school day starts again,
I have to stand out in the rain,
I'm soaked whilst I wait for my mate,
Standing still like a statue by the gate,
Been standing still for quite a while,
Here comes my best mate called Kyle,
We get ready for the new day,
Then suddenly Kyle runs away,
At 3.30 we all leave school,
And no one has broken a school rule,
We have to come back tomorrow,
And we are all filled with sorrow.

Dean Fletcher (11)
Landau Forte College

My First Day

F rightened,
I n a rush,
R eady?
S cared, more like
T errified.

D ay begins,
A nyone want to be my friend?
Y es!

A bit lost,
T ook the wrong turn.

L unchtime - *pizza!*
A fternoon seems very long,
N early home time,
D ay ends,
A nxiety,
U nnecessary!

Peter Temple (11)
Landau Forte College

My First Day Of School

I got on the bus on my first day of school,
I was very nervous about breaking a rule,
When I got to school, there was a lot of fuss,
I was even more nervous now than I
Had been when I got on the bus,
Year 7s were told to go into the theatre,
Big and wondrous, then Mr Witely came in
And started to talk to us,
As it got later in the day,
I started to settle in,
I felt more relaxed.

Thomas Roethenbaugh (11)
Landau Forte College

Of All!

Of all the words to say,
You use a gun,
Of all the words to speak,
You kill!

Of all the things to do,
You go to war,
Of all the things to write,
You sign that paper.

Of all the things to die for,
You die killing innocent people,
Of all the things to live for,
You live for war and destruction.

Of all the things to do now,
You still fight,
The thing to do now
Is to talk.

Kaylie Scattergood (14)
Landau Forte College

Nerve Station

The first day of school seemed to go really slow,
It seemed so complex that I wanted to go!
But as the day went by, things turned around,
The last hour started, lifting off the ground!

I got pushed around, had the locker on the floor,
Found it very hard to push open the doors!
But as I walked home, I thought, *what a great day*!
Now I can go home and shop on ebay.

Kirsty Tomlinson (12)
Landau Forte College

To Walk To Death

A gas shell shrieks to a halt,
Behind us it explodes,
We dive,
Up we get,
Onwards we trudge,
We are ill with fatigue,
At home our girls are waiting,
Forever they shall wait,
Their patience sweet,
As the hyacinth in bloom,
Of which I barely remember,
A tear to the eye,
It brings to us,
We will never set eyes on them again,
We are deaf,
Deaf to the sounds,
Of screeching rifles,
Setting ablaze the Onyx above,
Blind of pain we are,
Eyes weeping,
As the open wounds upon us do,
People drop down around us,
Collapsing, writhing, shaking,
We do not flinch,
For with the demons of hell,
We will go into battle,
An endless conflict,
We are numb,
Our eyes can only see the light now,
And we trudge onwards,
To our deaths.

Hayley Gaskin (14)
Landau Forte College

War Rap

What a waste of life,
Worry and strife,
Blair's lies,
His deceitful eyes,
Blood shed,
Too many people dead,
Babes at eighteen,
Recruited but not keen,
Off to pastures 'green',
To kill people unseen,
Bush too,
Telling us what we should do,
No true reasons why,
Just light up the sky,
A terrorist attack,
Giving us our anthrax back,
Has the world gone whack?
We want our soldiers back,
Politicians and bad guys,
Pull the wool over our eyes,
They're all the same it seems,
Destroying all the world's dreams.

Lewis Aldridge (13)
Landau Forte College

My New Life

In the London life, it was warm and miserable,
In the Derby life, it's cold and peaceful,
As I meet new people over here,
I still see people over there,
But as I settle down here,
There is no hope for me over there.

Katy Heap (12)
Landau Forte College

I'm In Liverpool Now

I'm in Liverpool now,
I arrived yesterday,
I came from Derby,
Although I wanted to stay.

I'm in Liverpool now,
Everything's changed,
It's so different here,
My life's rearranged.

I'm in Liverpool now,
It's not that bad,
I've made new friends,
But I miss the others I had.

I'm in Liverpool now,
The accent is weird,
It's hard to understand,
It's just like I feared.

I'm in Liverpool now,
It's kind of fun,
I can't wait to tell my friends,
All the things that I've done.

I'm in Liverpool now,
It feels like home,
But my old life's still part of me,
I feel happy not alone.

Kalisha Hamilton (12)
Landau Forte College

Start Of A New School!

As I walked through the dark, dingy cave,
I saw all the new Year 7s, trying to be brave,
As I crept through the crowded corridor,
Where everyone was staring,
And everyone was glaring,
As I heard the head lion roar,
That all Year 7s to wait by the door,
I went to my locker which was dull and empty,
But I looked at the others, they were full and plenty,
I went in a room, it was bright and airy,
I sat at a table, it wasn't so scary,
I met some of the natives,
They were quite friendly,
It came to the end of the day,
I said after three, *hip, hip, hooray!*

Stephanie Fox (12)
Landau Forte College

Landau Forte College

Days long
Corridors busy
Pencils and pens dash
Lockers jam
Gathering long
Teachers angry
Pencils snap
Playtime starts
People chattering
People laughing
Playtime ends
Lessons start
Back to work
At Landau Forte College.

Sam West (11)
Landau Forte College

School Limericks

Maths
Maths, it is a bore,
The students just ignore,
The teacher starts talking,
The students start walking,
They go out and slam the door!

Geography
Geography I'm not so sure about,
I'll give it the benefit of the doubt,
Reading the maps,
Fun? Perhaps,
If we get to go out!

PE
PE is good and great,
But something I really hate,
Is that silly old dance,
It's just so pants,
The teacher keeps us in late!

English
English helps you a lot,
It tells you to use a full stop,
The teacher keeps telling,
To practice your spellings,
Or else we all lose the plot!

Jordan Kelly (11)
Landau Forte College

A New Atmosphere

Of course on my first day Landau seemed massive,
My attitude was not to be passive,
I felt small, just like a mouse,
What I would give to be back at my house.

As soon as I got there, I held my breath,
Just think, I thought, *it's not your death,*
I stood outside standing aside,
And then I was told to go inside.

Into the theatre I was led,
I looked around and raised my head,
Up the steps I trampled slowly,
No one else seemed so lowly.

The principal gave a detailed speech,
And I was daydreaming of lying on a beach,
When he was finished, we journeyed to our room,
And I was filled with my gloom.

We looked at our student guide,
And eventually I began to push aside,
The misery that I'd started with,
And at Landau I started to live.

The shyness that had once consumed me,
Had been and gone, immediately,
Landau Forte seemed to get smaller,
And hey presto, I got taller.

The older pupils always called us cute,
But after a while, they began to mute,
Landau has become closer to me,
And after a while, it will seem normal,
You'll see!

Ellis Hannah Thorpe (11)
Landau Forte College

Memories Of The Past And Present

When I look back at St George's school,
I remember the things that were really cool,
When I look back it went so fast,
All the way to Year 6, the very last,
The thing I remember is all my friends,
I'll remember them forever, until the end.

When I started Landau Forte School,
I was in my uniform, I looked odd, I was a fool,
When I started, I felt so scared,
All the years looked at me, laughed and jeered,
But after 3 or 4 weeks,
I finally came down firmly on my feet.

Now I'm here at Landau Forte College,
Learning stuff and building up my knowledge,
Now I'm really enjoying it here,
My confidence has moved up a gear.

But one thing I'll remember about my old school,
Is all my friends.

But most importantly,
I like my friends,
They're just so much good fun,
I want these last 7 years to last forever.

Joseph Thorpe (11)
Landau Forte College

My School Poem

It's time for school,
It's going to be cool,
I can hang around with my best mate,
And I hope I'm not going to be late,
All my mates hate school,
But I think it's really cool!

Mark Woodward (12)
Landau Forte College

School Memories

In Landau Forte College,
I know that you will find,
People new and exciting,
Or people new and kind.

Your PT and your buddy tutor,
Are there when you need help,
So if you're stuck and upset,
Just give a little yelp.

You go into the canteen,
And collect your lovely lunch,
So get there before anyone else,
So you can have a munch.

Basketball and tennis,
Hockey, football too,
We do these in all sorts of weather,
So you'll need a very hot brew.

Some things you'll really enjoy,
Some things you'll want to lay rest,
So come to Landau Forte College,
And be the very best.

Frances Martin (12)
Landau Forte College

Looking Back

I was the shark in my old school,
But now I am the tadpole,
Swimming in this vast ocean,
Of lanky eighteen-year-olds.

My old school was a fish bowl,
And this feels like an ocean,
So big, so vast, crammed with students,
Easy to get totally lost!

Tom Buckner (11)
Landau Forte College

School Memories

The rushing of the corridors,
Kids blaring and kids swearing,
Lockers bashed, children pushing,
Strange new faces, kids tall and kids small,
The laughing of pranks and the tutors glaring,
Rules broken and discipline spoken,
No friends at first, now friends forever,
Swipe cards swaying, bags rushed,
Rolling of eyes at the tutor's pep talk,
Lunchtimes are packed with the smell of food,
Kids gobble and chatter or have friendly natter,
The conveyer belt jingling with cups and trays,
As the next lesson begins all that happens,
Kids daydream and doodle,
And all the kids think about is, *is it the end of the day?*
When they can have a break, run around and play.

Heather Dobbs (11)
Landau Forte College

My School Poem!

Up and out in such a rush,
Down the road to chase the bus,
The same old faces pass me by,
Will I get there while it's still dry?
It's Monday morning, the week's just started,
What's that smell, has someone farted?
We all go in, we heard the bell,
Let's hope this week's not hell,
We start with English, a spelling test,
I must listen hard to beat the rest,
Then it's maths, subtraction and divide,
On to algebra, it's time to hide,
Soon it's dinner and time to chat,
Who fancies who and all of that.

Anna Kingwell (12)
Landau Forte College

School

Scratching pens,
Chewed Biros,
Blunt pencils,
Keyboards tapping,
'Stop rocking on that chair!'
Chewing gum banned,
Teachers shouting,
Corridors busy,
Breaks short,
Lessons boring,
Daydreaming,
Window gazing,
Pages turning,
Fans whirring,
Sun burning,
Dinner queues long,
We haven't got long,
Stop pushing!
Don't run,
Teachers groaning,
Pupils moaning,
Not long left,
Home time soon,
Extra homework,
Shouts of play outside,
I can't play,
An exhausting day,
This is what I think of school!

Michael Wood (11)
Landau Forte College

My New School

First day of my new school,
I hope I don't look like a fool.
Bit of argy-bargy getting through the corridors,
Someone's pushed me from behind, ending up on all-fours.
Getting on time for my lesson, as the clock ticks by,
Any later, I might cry,
Opening my watering eyes to see the beautiful sun,
I knew it, I knew it, the boring lesson has begun.

Big people blaring and swearing as though they are talking Japanese,
More work piling up, I'm falling on my knees,
Different subjects remind me of a radiant colour,
These lessons are getting more and more duller.

Getting lost as if I'm in a spiralling maze,
My head's spinning, I'm in a daze,
Going round and round, seeing the same faces,
Oh dear! I'm ending up in the same places.

Queuing up for dinner,
They better hurry up, because I'll get thinner,
Finding lockers hard to use,
Any longer, I'm going to blow my fuse,
Last but not least the teachers are polite,
Whereas students like to fight!

Hafizah Khatoon (11)
Landau Forte College

It's Hard To Think

It's hard to think,
That this rotting body,
Was once a man,
My brother, once.

It's beyond belief,
That yesterday,
He was walking the dog,
And wasn't ill at all.

It can't be right,
That just this morning,
He stormed out of the house,
After an argument.

It's not possible,
That he slipped and fell,
Even if there were witnesses,
He knew the area too well.

It's so illogical,
He must have walked off,
Along a hidden path,
This isn't him, I know it isn't.

It's obvious he's faking,
He's hiding by the river,
I swear I can see him
He'll come out soon.

Jagraaj Dhammi (13)
Landau Forte College

Our Teacher

Our teacher's like no other teacher we've seen
She still likes to wear clothes from last Hallowe'en
While shouting at Tim, she will fall over her broom
Then our laughter will fill the room.

She is always losing her chalk
Which she throws at us if we should talk
She laughs at the mice inside the cage
But we have to do our work page by page

She loves to make us lovely jam tarts
She can be nasty but she's loved in our hearts
As for homework, we have no say
If it's not handed in she still lets us go play.

Our teacher is completely insane
Or some kind of genius with oodles of brain
But whether it's madness or strange powers
We don't think it matters, we're glad that she's ours.

James Capps (11)
Landau Forte College

I Miss . . .

I miss my old school quite a bit,
I miss the dinners, the cheese, the chips,
I miss the fun of my school,
I miss my friends, they were cool,
I miss the lessons, English, maths,
I miss the giggles, the chuckles, the laughs,
I miss the librarian, she was mad,
I miss the little kids, they were sad,
I miss the assemblies, they were boring,
I miss the Year 5s, who were snoring,
I miss the time when we did spellings,
I miss the howls, everyone was yelling!
I miss the time when I sighed,
I miss the last day when I cried.

Raheela Hussain (12)
Landau Forte College

The Pain, The Death, The Sorrow And The Mourning

In my heart I wither with pain,
My mind and body are going insane,
I cannot see your beautiful face,
I'm blind to the world, I'm in disgrace,
Blacked out from this world, I no longer see,
The happiness of you and me!
My body rests in its sacred crypt,
I only pray so you let me live for a longer bit,
My soul is released into the heavens above,
As I deport this Earth, I float like a dove,
I see mourning faces down below,
I no longer live, I don't feel this sorrow,
The look of death in my mother's eyes,
I see her, I feel her, I hear her cries.

Rose Akers (14)
Landau Forte College

Starting School

Starting school is very scary,
You feel like a little fairy,
Walking round this big fat school,
Trying not to break any rules,
So everything is going fine,
And everyone is so kind,
So that is the end of my first day,
And everything went OK.

Danielle Randle (11)
Landau Forte College

Landau Forte

Landau Forte is the best,
Away and ahead of all the rest,
Now I enjoy going to school,
Day 3, week 1 is so cool,
A sandwich at dinner is so nice,
Unusual treats never cease to entice.

Full of friendly clever tutors,
Oh, looking around there are no looters,
Reading a book in tutor time,
Trying in drama to do a mime,
Everything in Landau is so great,
The lessons are fun so don't be late!

David Wilson (10)
Landau Forte College

Cool School!

It's time for school,
Today it will be cool,
We have got a test,
And it's bound to be a pest,
You cannot cheat,
Or you will be dead meat,
You need to revise,
So you can rise,
Up in school
And that, is cool!

Connor Boylan (11)
Landau Forte College

All Grown Up

Now that I have started secondary school,
I thought, *OK this is cool,*
When I was wandering round this school,
I needed some company, not just me,
So I met this great friend called Cherie!

I thought secondary was gonna be tough,
But now I just can't get enough,
The lessons are good, the teaches are fun,
Joining dance class is the best thing I ever have done.

So coming to Landau Forte School,
Is just so massively cool!

Aisha Roberts (11)
Landau Forte College

School

The corridors packed full,
My friends start to pull,
What's my next class?
The time seems to pass,
What shall I eat?
Where's my seat?
The day has now passed,
It never seems to last!

Cassandra Duncan (11)
Landau Forte College

First Day At School!

The classrooms are so boring,
The lockers are so dull,
The rating for the toilets,
Will just have to be null!

The children's language is so sickening,
The dinner's price is so high,
At my first day at school,
I thought I had to say bye!

I made a few friends,
Who were quite good,
Looking at children who grew so tall,
Like a flower from a bud!

Just when I got used to it,
It all went down the drain,
I lost my timetable, left my book
And the teachers went insane!

The teachers speak gibberish,
The children are just geeks,
The Year 8s are so nasty,
And always call us freaks!

The Year 10s have their top buttons undone,
And think they're so cool,
The most tragic day of my entire life . . .
Was my first day at school!

Jagjeevan Johal (11)
Landau Forte College

School!

Corridors are cramped as if trapped in a cage,
Crouching down low to get to lockers, as if the
                                    ceilings have lowered,
The fear of having no friends, I have been thrown
                            into a chamber, all alone.

My nerves cracking at the thought of
Going up, gathering butterflies in my stomach.

Pushed to India, shoved to Pakistan as though I am a
Message in a bottle.

Glaring at the teacher, she's my enemy.

The squeaking of the board pen is as if I have
Mice squeaking below my toes.

Always staying out of the way of older kids,
They are a threat to us.

The excitement of being treated as younger
Adults as though I am royalty.

The thought of piles of homework to go through
In one night, is as if my freedom has floated away.

Wondering whether going to school is worth it,
It is as though I am the Queen wondering what decision to make.
Oh yeah, school's just great!

Taibah Yasin (11)
Landau Forte College

Rainbow

When I first stepped onto this plain of feeling,
I marvelled at the strength and speed,
Of this fierce emotion clapped in irons.
On love and power, I once did feed,
Gorging myself without regret or thought.
I perhaps began this thoughtful seed,
A chain of pleasure, pain and greed.

When I first stepped onto this plain of needing,
I never knew it could sting me so,
Whiplash; a recoil of numbing agony,
I curled up, foetal, hid from the blow,
My chest split in two, split by thunder and fire.
I wept like a fool and pressed down so low,
Clinging to memories I hated to know.

My shattered mirror is repaired, like new,
A shining reflection of life and new hope.
Cruelty's hand has been slapped away,
No longer to grip at my life, nor to grope,
For the love that you give me, no longer to steal.
Warm and soft, caressing like gold, a rope,
Never-ending of heat and new plains.

Lucy Stanton-Greenwood (16)
Netherthorpe School

My World

The tears roll painfully
Down the side of my face
While shivers race rapidly
Like the burning of flames
Up the whole of my body
Without leaving a trace.

Then I'll close my eyes
And drift slowly away
To a place where I'm safe
Away from reality.

Away from my fears
Away from the pain
Away from the heartache
Of not seeing you again
When I'm here I'm so happy
All my problems are solved
I can laugh
I can smile
I can be me for a while.

I don't have to be well-mannered
I don't have to be polite
I don't have to say thank you
And yes that's very nice
I can tell people where to shove it
If by chance I disagree
And now I love you even more
Because you've freed the inner me.

Now I wish I could say more but my time has nearly gone.
I'm awakening from this dream
But my world will still last on
Now remember me for me
Like I've remembered you
And remember that
I will always love you
And if you ever need me
Do this one important thing
Close your eyes
Think deeply
And there in my world
I will be.

Jody Robinson (15)
Netherthorpe School

Everyone's Destruction!

This is a charm to cause utmost fear,
This is a charm to shed a tear,
For this is a potion of a fearsome sort,
One which will make Earth's population decrease to nought.

For thy charm will revive a demon king,
For his scythe is as terrible as a sting,
The guardian of Hell and the gate keeper,
For the charm will summon the Grim Reaper.

And for thy charm in must go,
Hair of wolf and dead man's toe,
Sheep's eye and a horse's heart,
A pint of blood and a poison dart.

Dead lizard's leg and a bat's wing,
Monkeys' brains and a wild wasp's sting,
Now this charm is surely done,
Killing everyone sure is fun!

Johnathan Curd (13)
Noel-Baker Community School & Language College

A Charm For Eternal Life

Onion juice and skin of peaches,
Rose petals and slim of leeches,
Cup of sunshine and pinch of mud,
Brown sauce and antennae of slug,
Chop it up, throw in a pan,
Go outside wait for a tan.

Blue ink and large toenails,
Frog's skin and shells of snails,
Toadstools and wing of bat,
Fluff from a teddy bear's hat,
Mix it up, watch it bubble,
Hubble bubble tar and trouble.

Pot of salt and metal spoon,
Sugar cube and scream of doom,
Lump of coal and sprinkle of bugs,
Blood of snake and bowl of wood,
Pour in a jar, wait three months,
After that - drink! *Mind the lumps!*

Samantha Kemp (12)
Noel-Baker Community School & Language College

A Magical Night

F iery volcanoes fill the night,
I ndigo fireworks, flashes of light.
R ockets zoom into the air,
E ntertaining people everywhere.
W hizzing sounds of the Catherine wheel,
O rganic oranges for our meal.
R ippling flames of the bonfire,
K ings and queens gaze up higher and higher.
S afe and sound in my bed as the light of the bonfire dies away.

Shellie Morgan (12)
Noel-Baker Community School & Language College

Ice Cream Scream!

Add two scoops of ice,
That'll make it really nice,
Flower petals in for fun,
Hair of a holy nun,

> Whip up cream,
> Crush the ice,
> Add a scream,
> And headlice.

Toss up like a pancake,
Put it in to bake,
Grate some cheese,
Add some green peas.

> Whip up cream,
> Crush the ice,
> Add a scream,
> And headlice.

Fluffy as a big white cloud,
Make not even the smallest sound,
Add a summer's breeze,
And an old man's sneeze.

> Whip up cream,
> Crush the ice,
> Add a scream,
> And headlice.

Last of all zebra hair,
Far from a bear's lair,
Add an evil man's plot,
And a happy lady's flowerpot.

> Screams and trouble
> Are on the double.

Zoe Handley (12)
Noel-Baker Community School & Language College

Chocolate Charm

Add in your bowl a Kit-Kat,
Then a Bounty nice and flat,
Add a Freddo, two or three,
Throw in a chocolate key,
Put in a bar of chocolate cream,
Let the melted chocolate flow like a stream.

Put in the oven for one hour,
Mix in the bowl with all your power,
Sprinkle chocolate crumbs over the top,
Then add one little chocolate drop,
For half an hour, leave to stand,
Eat up and you'll be in chocolate land.

Becky Keeling-Brown (12)
Noel-Baker Community School & Language College

A Good Luck Charm

Into the lucky pot we put,
A crystal ball and a rabbit's foot,
Mix in a number 7, add a colourful rainbow,
Blend it with some glitter and away we go.

Sprinkle some dust from a unicorn's horn,
And seal it with luck from a leprechaun,
Chop up some crystals and sprinkle it in,
And from then on let the magic begin.

A dash of stars, the hint of a moon,
The heat of the sun, in the afternoon,
A touch of clovers, throw in a horseshoe,
Good luck to last you, all year though!

Catherine Huynh (12)
Noel-Baker Community School & Language College

Chocoholic's Charm

If you're a chocoholic,
This poem won't make you feel sick,
It's all about chocolate,
So make sure that you like it.

First you'll need a gigantic pot,
Throw in some chocolate shots,
Break up a Twirl,
Then give it a swirl,
If you like Kit-Kat,
Make sure you put in that.

Chocolate Buttons are yummy,
They fill up your tummy,
Add them to the spell,
But make sure you don't tell,
Throw in a Twix,
Then give it a mix.

Drop in a Toblerone,
Like you have been shown,
Mix in a Lion Bar,
You should make a puff of stars,
Throw in now, a chocolate Flake,
But make sure it doesn't break.

It's important to add a Dairy Milk,
If you melt it, it feels like silk,
So if you put in some Quality Street,
Now the charm is really complete,
Have some twice, every week,
This is the charm, you seek.

Charlotte Adamsons (12)
Noel-Baker Community School & Language College

Things Happen

Teddy is singing,
Not too high,
He thought he was blinking,
Out of sight.

Tigers are roaring,
Not too loud,
The rain is pouring from the cloud.

Bees are buzzing, everywhere,
On the ground and in the air.

People are walking on the road,
I saw a boy with a bag of gold.

Snakes are slithering on the ground,
In the air and right back down.

Dogs are barking, day and night,
One of them gave me a
Big fright!

Nits are crawling in your head,
They are there when you go to bed.

Swans are swimming in the sea,
Water is moving, that's how it's meant to be.

Samera Parveen Saghir (11)
Noel-Baker Community School & Language College

A Recipe For Love

I sat down one day
And a bundle of love jumped on my knee.
I looked down and it was my puppy,
I saw it looking up at me,
I thought it was so funny,
It has only got one master,
And that is me, my loveable puppy.

Chelsea Carr (12)
Noel-Baker Community School & Language College

Witches' Chant!

Round about the cauldron go,
In the dead rats' mucus throw,
Red raw eyes have bloody veins,
Small dead rodents' squished brains,
Boil though first in the charmed pot,
Double, double, boil and trouble,
Fire burn and cauldron bubble.

Fillet of a phoenix feather,
In the cauldron boil together,
Tail of a cat and a tongue of a frog,
A blind worm's sting and a brain of a dog,
A crocodile's tooth and a python's fork,
Horses' legs and a baby's talk,
For a charm of powerful trouble,
Like a hell - broth boil and bubble,
Double, double, toil and trouble,
Fire burn and cauldron bubble.

Jack Kay (11)
Noel-Baker Community School & Language College

A Recipe For A Friend!

All you need is to be kind,
A bit of fun would be nice,
All you need is to ask their name,
And then you are best of friends.

Best friends, silly friends, mad friends,
Normal friends, stupid friends.

All you need is to be nice,
A bit of stupidness would be good,
All you need is to be their friend,
And then you are best of friends.

Best friends, kind friends, cool friends,
Wicked friends, super friends.

Nicole Kelly (11)
Noel-Baker Community School & Language College

A Good Luck Spell

Mix a horseshoe,
With a Dalmatian's spot,
A four leaf clover
And boil it to make it hot.

A loving heart,
A new baby just born,
Eeyore's eyes,
And new freshly picked corn.

A bucket of cold water,
To cool it down,
Lots of loving kisses,
To say you're loved around.

A row of a boat,
A dolphin's fin,
A squeeze cuddle,
To say you're loved within.

Take a pinch of wishes,
And then mix it well,
Stir it with flowers,
And you've finished your good luck spell.

Sarah Richards (13)
Noel-Baker Community School & Language College

Love

Candlelight lit in the corner,
Chocolates waiting to be eaten,
Flower lovely blowing in the wind,
Love letters waiting to be read,
A lingering meal being eaten,
As the beautiful night draws in.

Stacey-Anne Marshall (12)
Noel-Baker Community School & Language College

Perfect Spell

Ten witches round the cauldron go,
A puppy's eye, a baby's toe,
Throw in spice, and throw in blood,
Throw in everything pure and good,
Put in a beggar, add a nun,
Put in the crumbs of a mouldy bun.

Mix it together, quick and well,
This will give you the perfect spell!

A kitten's paw, a raven's claw,
Makes the spell just that much more,
A lamb killed in the dead of the night,
A newborn calf that died of fright,
Tail of mouse and fangs of snake,
Hair of toddler, drowned in a lake.

Mix it together quick and well,
This will give you the perfect spell!

Amy Bates (13)
Noel-Baker Community School & Language College

Happiness

Take the sunset and the stars,
The colours of the rainbow,
Add the sparkle of the sea,
See how happy you can be,
Smiling faces, happy place,
A child's hope and lots of love,
Birds singing up above,
Stir it up and fill with glee,
Flames flickering in the breeze,
A fresh red rose picked at noon,
Hope and peace are coming soon.

Heather Bull (12)
Noel-Baker Community School & Language College

A Charm For Bullies

In the poison I will throw
The ear of a dog,
In it will go.
In the poison I will throw
The tail of a cat, in it will go.
Chop and stir the wing of an eagle,
And send it to that barking beagle,
Then mix in that stupid seagull,
Then add in that cheeky child,
Then the teacher as well to make it mild,
Why not the tongue of a bull and the old man's skull,
The arm of an angry hulk,
Just to make that old witch sulk,
And then why not the toe of a newborn baby,
But then again, you might get them nasty scabies:

Kimberley Moore (11)
Noel-Baker Community School & Language College

Revenge

Round about the cauldron go,
In the deadly spiders throw,
Sting of a scorpion, under the pot,
Heart of a baby, without a safe cot,
For a charm of powerful trouble,
Like hell broth boil and bubble.
Fillet of a maggot's gut,
Throw in a dead tiger's foot,
Screech of a falcon, wing of an owl,
Nothing tastes that good, all is foul,
For a charm of powerful trouble,
Like hell broth boil and bubble.

Megan Warren (12)
Noel-Baker Community School & Language College

Fear And Fright

Paw of lion, wing of bat,
Add in live mouse and dead cat,
Spiders fang full of venom,
Sourness of a lemon.

For a spell of hideous fear,
Add a scream that everyone can hear,
Make blood flow, free as a river,
Place in kidney, and liver,
Deadly disease to dampen life,
Heart of duck, cut out with knife.

Chloë Martin (12)
Noel-Baker Community School & Language College

We Shall Put In The Cauldron

The hooves of a fawn, that we will put in at dawn,
And the venom of a silver snake,
The spikes of a thistle tree and the key to the castle of doom,
The howl of a midnight wolf,
Who cries at the start of dawn,
Those are the things we put in for lunch,
So we can have a jolly good munch.

Amy Pincock (13)
Noel-Baker Community School & Language College

Peace

In my potion, I will add . . .
Smiling faces, people glad,
Morning sunshine, midnight stars,
First born baby, gifts and cards,
Happiness and lots of love,
Teddy bears and one big hug.

Aimee Cummins (12)
Noel-Baker Community School & Language College

The Hatred Spell

Eye of newt,
Tail of rat,
All mixed up with the brains of a bat,
Nose of sprog,
Ears of humans,
All mixed up with the fleas of a dog,
Spider's leg, to give it that kick,
Hamster's tongue,
And monkey's sick.
Just to make it that little bit worse,
The best ingredients from my curse.
Bats
Unicorns
Ghosts
Snakes.

Garret Johnston
Noel-Baker Community School & Language College

Spells

Spells, spells, witches' spells,
Doctors' spells for science,
Spells that make you fall in love,
And spells that stop all violence.

Spells, spells, all around,
You never know they're there,
Always helping people love,
Like cupid in the air.

Spells, spells, that no one likes,
The spells that are for evil,
Poison in a lizard pie,
Could destroy all people.

Sophie Brown (12)
Noel-Baker Community School & Language College

Witches Everywhere!

Witches, witches everywhere,
Swooping around with long black hair,
Cast a spell here, cast a spell there,
Add a leg,
And a leaf of a hedge,
A spider from a window ledge.

Witches, witches everywhere,
Swooping around with long black hair,
Now add a frog,
And a nose from a hog,
And hose it down with a deep brown log.
Add some meat,
And a little heat.

Witches, witches everywhere.

Emma Druce (12)
Noel-Baker Community School & Language College

Evil

Doggy's tongue and cat's tail long,
In they put the gore and blood,
Blind man's hands and baby's leg,
Manky green swamp in a flood.

Stir it up with an evil spell,
Pop and squeak goes the cauldron hell,
Slobber from a dog, dirt too,
Dracula's teeth, witch's nose,
Loud green rattlesnake's poison,
In goes the baby's head.
Dead!

Sophie Harrison (12)
Noel-Baker Community School & Language College

A Recipe For Disaster

The graveyard gates were locked at 10,
But they didn't worry,
The witches scaled the iron walls,
In something of a hurry.

They stood the cauldron on the grave,
Of their dear departed,
Around the pot they kneeled and then,
All at once they started . . .

A pint of blood they put in first,
Then a warty frog,
A lizard's leg and owl's beak,
A bloody tongue of dog.

They stirred the mixture round and round,
Until it all turned green,
Then they added yet more blood,
And mouldy clotted cream.

Paw of cat and toe of hog,
They added to the pot,
Heart of boy and brain of girl,
Fungus, mould and rot.

One more stir to mix it up -
The mixture turned bright red,
The witches drank it one by one,
And soon all three were dead!

James Heathcote (13)
Noel-Baker Community School & Language College

My First Day

'Ohh you're going to school now,' said my mum
'Big school!'
Why did she call it big school?
Was it very big?
'And you're going to wear a tie and blazer,'
Tie and blazer!
Don't posh men wear blazers?

Going up the drive is scary,
Maybe big school isn't that good,
Maybe I should just go home and play
On the computer,
'No,' Mum said, Ali and Jonathan would look after me,
But where have they gone?

'Hello are you in 7N?'
7N what's that? Sounds like a room number,
'You're in room 301, OK?'
301 where's that?
'Go and line up then,'
Line up where, I don't like this . . .
There's Jonathan maybe he will help me!

The end of the day has come,
It wasn't that bad,
But tomorrow I've got to put more money on my dinner card,
With the strange machine.

Christina Lewis (12)
Queen Elizabeth's Grammar School

Industry

They come with machines,
Sharp, jagged and cruel,
They cut, hack and saw,
Greed willing them on,
Money feeding their hunger,
Menacing teeth of blades gnarling
At bark.

They never learn -
Floods, quakes and storms punish,
But never teach,
They leave nothing, only roots, stumps of betrayal,
Leaves and bark burn, sap on fire,
Sawdust flies as weapons are mustered.

Moulded into unnatural household items,
Final stages take place,
Through shop windows they stare -
Hands clutching notes and coins.

They never put back,
Permanent damage smothers acres of once lush land,
They don't stop, unfairness never will,
It's a terrible thing -
Industry - one true weapon of mass destruction.

Emily Smith (13)
Queen Elizabeth's Grammar School

Animals

The little kitten
Sits in the tall, high branches,
Watching and waiting.

The playful puppy,
Running, jumping and catching,
Chasing the ball.

The waddling penguin,
Sliding down slippery slopes,
Catching fish for tea.

The cute white rabbit,
Nibbles at lettuce at lunch,
Has floppy ears.

The colourful fish,
Swimming calmly in the tank,
Nibbling at fish food.

The slimy snail,
Slithers across the pavement,
Taking up his time.

The slithering snake,
Creeping slyly up the trees,
Looking for its prey.

Hannah Smith (11)
Queen Elizabeth's Grammar School

Funny Poems

There was a man from Derby,
Who had a doll called Barbie,
He said, 'Boo!'
Then the Barbie went down the loo,
That silly old man from Derby.

There was a man who was called Pat,
He had a best friend who was fat,
There was another friend called Billy,
Then they all started being silly,
So they all went home for tea.

There was a girl called Leanne,
She had a friend called Diane,
They both had an apple,
Then they had egg scrabble,
Then they went to sleep with a sheep.

There was a man riding a donkey,
Then this girl started being cocky,
Then she had her tea,
Then she went back down the sea,
That silly girl who was being cocky.

Leanne Cheshire (12)
Queen Elizabeth's Grammar School

Old Men

There was an old man from Taiwan,
Who loved to drink out of a can,
He opened some fizz,
That sent him in a whizz,
That stupid old man from Taiwan.

There is also a man from France,
Who loved to sing and dance,
He danced to the moon,
And made a baboon,
That frightened the people of France.

Grant Blenkinsop (12)
Queen Elizabeth's Grammar School

Fleas As White As Snow

(Based on 'Mary Had A Little Lamb')

Mary had a little lamb,
Little lamb, little lamb,
Mary had a little lamb
With fleas as white as snow.

And everywhere that Mary went,
Mary went, Mary went,
Everywhere that Mary went,
Those fleas were sure to go.

They followed her to school one day,
School one day, school one day,
They followed her to school one day,
In time for show and tell.

They made the children scratch away,
Scratch away, scratch away,
They made the children scratch away,
And Mary got expelled.

Natasha Coates (11)
Queen Elizabeth's Grammar School

Love A Dog

I have a dog called Jessie,
We go on lots of exciting walks,
Every day,
And we always have lots of interesting talks.

We go over the hills and far away,
Through swamps and the odd dirty bog,
We fight our way through jungles and forests,
And jog through the misty fog.

Katherine Smith (11)
Queen Elizabeth's Grammar School

Chapel Poem

A candle was going crackle,
In a nearby chapel,
Some books were open on their page,
To sing so as not to make God rage,
And on the desk stood a golden goblet,
With carved-in ferrets around the side,
And as my eyes opened wide,
I saw on top of a rope, a bell,
Which would be rather heavy if it fell,
And round the sides were some windows of glass,
So dazzling I still wonder why they were covered up like masks,
And in the corner stood a wooden cross,
Laden with plants and shrubs including moss,
Around Jesus' head was a ring of thorns,
Which from a distance looked like horns,
And round his legs was a thin white cloth,
Which attracted quite a few little moths.

It is tomorrow and I'm back at the chapel,
And guess what . . . the candle is still going crackle.

Heather Hughes (11)
Queen Elizabeth's Grammar School

Nose Dive

There was a young pilot from Crewe,
Who bought a jet plane, which he flew,
The nose took a dive,
He crashed, but survived,
And now he drives a Daihatsu.

Matthew Kingdon (11)
Queen Elizabeth's Grammar School

Beyond The Madness

The waste of living
The taste of insanity
Being eaten alive by this damn democracy
Always knowing what it's like
Being inside a twisted mind.

Beyond the madness
You could seek out the happiness
Your strategy just fallen apart
Below the surface your future has swollen
What have I done to deserve this?

One smashed window
A broken chair
Just a few small things that you couldn't spare
My life is long
But promised with despair,
So let me go
For I don't care.

Amy Allcock (12)
Queen Elizabeth's Grammar School

The Natural World

Giraffes wander through the bush,
Crickets disturb the hush,
Elephants gather together,
They don't mind the wet weather,
Monkeys sit and eat bananas,
In a nearby tree, you can see koalas,
Families of lions kill and eat,
Vultures feed on the leftover meat,
Pandas eating bamboo,
Cheetah's closing in on an antelope
What should it do?

Mark Coxon (11)
Queen Elizabeth's Grammar School

The Sea

Quiet as a millpond, glistening in the sun,
Children at the water's edge having lots of fun,
Little boats and dinghies sailing gently by,
Fathers with binoculars watch seagulls wheel and fly.

This week has ended, another on its way,
The sea is dark and angry, the sky dark and grey,
The waves crash down upon the rocks,
The waters foam and froth,
And when the tide is turning and the waters roll away,
The seaweed and the debris,
Are high up in the bay.

No one can control you
You are as you wish to be
You're a great mighty water
Just plainly called the sea.

Emily Taylor (11)
Queen Elizabeth's Grammar School

Dying In The War!

I see soldiers, cold and sick
    but still they go on,
Soldiers getting shot and dying
    but still the war goes on
Rats running, eating dead flesh
    but still the soldiers go on
Soldiers, slipping in the trenches
    but still the mud goes on
Soldiers hear others screaming and shouting
    but still the soldiers die
'Help, help, help!' they cry
    but war goes on and on and on.

Junior Morris-Varley (14)
St Clare's Special School, Derby

Kids

It's Christmas time,
I wish I was home
With my family
Watching the kids.
But I am here
In the trench.
Cold and hungry
Thinking of my kids.
I need to see them
My precious kids.

I hear the shot
Feel the pain
I know I will never
See my kids again.

Danny Moore (14)
St Clare's Special School, Derby

To My Sweetheart Sarah

I am 16 years old but feel 90
I wish I was home in good old Blighty.

I wish there was no war
Please stop now -
Please, no more!

Sarah is her name
I hope to see her again.
If I die and we are to part
Please dear Lord, look after my sweetheart.

Wesley Gregory (14)
St Clare's Special School, Derby

War Is So Cruel

When I was a soldier I thought about war
Gunfire, very loud
I was scared
But I am no more.

I stood in the trenches
My feet, cold and wet
Dead bodies everywhere
Making me cry.

We all march slowly
Our loads are heavy
Bombs explode
Cuts and burns all over my body.

Now I am home
My experience is over
Life goes on.

Musdiq Rizwan (15)
St Clare's Special School, Derby

Fear Of War

It is a starry night with softly blowing wind,
I hear tanks approaching,
I feel scared.
My heart is thumping,
I can hardly feel my feet,
I am desperate to see my girlfriend.
For two years we've been apart,
I want to hold her in my arms
And feel the beat of her heart.
The war started in 1914 and will be
Finished by Christmas
I want to be able to forget war.

Phillip Collinson (15)
St Clare's Special School, Derby

The Bomb Field

I am walking across the bomb field,
My friends are by my side.
The enemy is ahead,
One of my friends steps on a mine.
He's blown to pieces,
We all feel his pain.
We think of his family,
And the misery they will experience again.
It was bad enough to lose him,
When he went away to war.
Now they will never see him,
Come home to open the door.
The poppies are growing in the field,
So very red and so pretty,
They remind us of all the soldiers who have died
As all of us looked straight ahead, we cried.
His body lies on the ground,
We really have to leave him.
We all move forward to the trench,
Jump in and live another day.

War is so cruel.

Jamie John (14)
St Clare's Special School, Derby

War

W ater and mud
A mmunition
R ed like blood.

Simon Murney (14)
St Clare's Special School, Derby

Days In The Trenches

It's wet and cold and snowing,
fast guns in the distance then a loud blast.

It feels very strange in this foreign land,
but I'm not scared, my gun is at hand.

We're standing in mud in this terrible trench,
all around us, war's dreadful stench.

Clouds of smoke poison the air,
cries of the wounded, everywhere.

Suddenly the sun breaks through
lifting our spirits and cheering us too.

A new day dawns on this dreadful war
God give us the strength to face even more.

Daniel Schurian (15)
St Clare's Special School, Derby

Rotting Bodies

R ain flooding our trenches,
O ur best mates have died.
T he crackle and bang of
T he bombs in our ears.
I ntense screams come from the darkness.
N ight, never-ending.
G uns groaning.

B ombs banging
O ur feet aching.
D own in the dirty stench of the trench.
I cy winds nip at our hands and faces,
E veryone tries to keep warm.
S ad, sad endings.

Ian Wallis (14)
St Clare's Special School, Derby

Trenches

T renches, deep in slimy mud,
R ifles ringing single shots.
E ffort to walk through muddy fields.
N oise everywhere.
C raters full of blood and bones,
H orses dead and wounded.
E ach soldier cries out in pain,
S tarving with cold and hunger.

Jessica Munton (14)
St Clare's Special School, Derby

Soldier

S creaming soldiers crawling across the muddy floor,
O ver the creeping trenches, lie mouldy, dead bodies.
L ong, lonely nights they sleep in rain and snow, hunger gnawing.
D ark nights passing by, shooting guns, doesn't stop 'til day passes.
I ce-cold body, freezing in the snow.
E vil enemy scurrying around us, upon 'Open fire!'
R ats nibbling the rotten bodies lying in the slimy, dirty ditch.

Chantelle Morris (15)
St Clare's Special School, Derby

War

W hich soldiers will live?
A nd which will be killed?
R ussian, French or British?

Ashley Pipes (14)
St Clare's Special School, Derby

World War I

W orried mother because her son is going to war.
O utcry because their boys are dying.
R escued by nurses from the battlefields.
L onely soldiers, missing their parents.
D estroyed arms, legs, bodies and minds.

W ondering if they're alive or dead,
A ir is filled with gas and bullets.
R otting bodies, choking and burning.

O nly hope is to kill the enemy,
N obody liked the gas because it killed people.
E veryone has died.

Leonard Dolby (14)
St Clare's Special School, Derby

Trenches

T errible noises in my head
R ats running from the bombs,
E veryday tragedy in the war,
N ight-times are scary.
C areful not to smell the gas!
H ungry, only dry biscuits to eat.
E veryone feeling sad.
S oldiers fighting for England.

Flora Solomou (14)
St Clare's Special School, Derby

A Father

A father can be any man
A father is our Lord
A father will save you if he can
A father's not ignored.

A father is kind and caring
A father keeps you safe
A father's so amazing
A father gives you faith.

A father helps you out a lot
A father plays your games
A father raised you in a cot
A father is the greatest!

Jacob King (11)
St John Houghton RC School, Ilkeston

Long Gone

I look from the dark doorway
Of my old house,
I see the boy rushing after
His chestnut-brown dog.
I can smell the strong scent
Of freshly painted wood resin
And hear the occasional screeching
Of a car down the ink-black road.
There is also the high-pitched laughter
Of children playing in their secluded back garden.
And I see the smoking factories sheltered
Beneath the orange horizon.
Though these memories are all far behind me
They will never fade from my mind.

Leigh Davies (11)
The Ecclesbourne School

The View At Mirador

The little toy cars are trundling along the winding roads of La Graciosa
It is as if you're soaring right over the island.
You could just simply pick it up.
The deep azure-blue water, surrounding the island,
Calm as an extinct volcano, shines like jewels.
On the horizon, is a layer of steel-coloured mist,
Which hangs in the air like a bird of prey, waiting to drop.
The bare, chestnut-brown earth rises occasionally.
Into a sharply inclined volcano.
A strong scent of the Atlantic Ocean
Wafts through the air and fills your lungs.
The shrill sound of squawking seagulls and the crashing
Surf below, pound your ears.
On the pier, waiting for the ferry are tiny coloured dolls,
The size of pinpricks.

Joe Hoblyn (12)
The Ecclesbourne School

The Whale

The azure ocean laps at the boat,
I taste the tang of salty water.
As a breeze brushes my face,
There, in the distance, she swims,
A baby at her side.
Their bond is love itself.
The baby rolls and capers in the sea.
I'm so tempted to join in,
The mother is so careful
And tries to control her baby,
But he keeps slipping away.
For creatures of their size, they are gentle.
They swim silently,
Till their tails thrash the water,
Then they're gone.

Isabel Fleming (11)
The Ecclesbourne School

A View Of Paris

Standing on top of a huge metal jigsaw,
I gaze out at the marbled streets of Paris,
Reaching for miles around.

Scarlet-faced tourists, all staring in awe
At the ink-black valley dotted with golden light,
Brightening up the fantasy town below.

Breathing in the faint smell of fresh bread,
Which had drifted up thousands of feet
To greet us from the land below.

Miles above the ground, the bitter autumn breeze
Blows away my echoing thoughts
As I take in the once in a lifetime view
From the top of the Eiffel Tower.

Alice Lowe (12)
The Ecclesbourne School

The Return

The spotlights beam down,
The ball comes spinning,
Thudding on the orange-peel clay.
I'm all tensed up
On the balls of my feet.
My sticky palm grips the rubber handle.
Knees start to bend,
Racket swings back,
The ball arcs towards me.
My arm drives through
The strings come into contact -
Scraping on the frizzy surface.
Now it soars
Back to where it started,
And it's gone.

Charlie Pollard (11)
The Ecclesbourne School

Fierce I ams

I am . . .
The claret flame from the fire,
Twisting and turning, trying to reach out.
The fierce bark of a dog
Trying to get the attention of his owner.

I am . . .
The fizz from a drink can
Frothing all over the sides.
The crashing milky waves,
That tumble onto the sandy beaches.

I am . . .
The slam of the door
That rattles through the house.
The twist of the hurricane
That destroys life.

I am . . .
The thunder from a storm
Booming through the skies above.
The bang from the fireworks,
Like gunshots in the night.

Bethanie Ragsdell (12)
The Ecclesbourne School

Looking Out Of The Window

Looking out of the window
The silent tapping of the wind,
The clouds had parted
Leaving a brilliant golden sunbeam.
Bathing the soundless streets
Below, in an aura of divine holiness.
The shimmering, glossy raindrops
Held in place by sheets of searing light.
The milky-white clouds had linked again.

Christopher Watts (11)
The Ecclesbourne School

Tired I Ams

I am the cobwebs in the corner of the sitting room,
I am the bath, just seconds away from overflowing,
I am the cup of tea gradually getting colder,
I am the curtains still closed at midday.

I am the washing getting saturated in the rain,
I am the bookmark,
Which hasn't moved for weeks and weeks,
I am the ironing waiting tediously to be done.

I am the garden congested with weeds,
I am the dustbin brimming with garbage,
I am the clothes in a mountain on the floor,
I am the dirty plates and cups waiting to be washed.

I am the twinkle in the lights left on, when the sun is shining,
I am the grubby car waiting to be washed,
I am the windows covered in muck,
I am the toys strewn all over the house.

I am the dog, tiresomely waiting for a walk,
I am the shaggy old clothes waiting to be fixed,
I am the cooker covered in dirt,
I am the carpet needing a vacuum.

I am the floor in need of a scrub,
I am the half-decorated wall needing a lick of paint,
I am the shoes waiting to be polished,
I am the unfinished book, gathering dust.

Claire Cooper (12)
The Ecclesbourne School

Sad I Ams

I am . . .
The last crisp leaf, hanging from a tree,
The cold drip in an empty cup of tea.
The dog that nobody desires, seated behind bars,
The missing string off an abandoned guitar.

I am . . .
A light bulb that no longer shines,
The solitary hair, alone on the brush.
The olive-green egg which did not hatch,
A strip of sellotape, hardly visible on the chair.

I am . . .
The frayed stitch on a faded scarf,
The ball of sticky gum, immovable under the table,
The unwanted bean that slid off the plate,
The silver back of an earring, lost in the dust.

I am . . .
An ancient wooden doll, crumbling to the touch,
A rusted coin, down the deepest drain.
The last to be picked from my mother's litter,
The dull metallic lead that snapped off the pencil.

I am . . .
The last number, unwiped from the board,
The final page in the book,
The last word to be written.

Katherine Curley (12)
The Ecclesbourne School

Sad I Ams

I am the rusty bike wheel at the back of the garage,
The dead plant in the corner of the room
The key with no door.
The house with no family
The pet with no owner.

I am the boarded-up window
The unwanted teddy bear
The sharpened down pencil stub.
The unlit candle
The unseen play

I am the unread book
The ball that isn't bounced
The stale bread at the back of the cupboard,
The unheard voice.

Connor Rogers (12)
The Ecclesbourne School

Angry I Ams

I am the boy angry with the people who fight,
kill and starve others.
Angry that my bike was stolen.
I am the boy with the GameBoy but no games.
Angry that the car didn't start so I was late
and got detention.
I am the boy with the brother who picks on him.
Angry that his skateboard got run over.
I am the boy with the guitar which
mysteriously disappeared.
Angry that he has enemies, instead of friends.
I am the boy who will end this story
but it still goes on and on.

Zack Oxley (12)
The Ecclesbourne School

Sad I Ams

I am . . .
The embers from a burnt out fire
The unread letter received last year
The creaking door not yet oiled
A one-eyed teddy stuffed under the bed

I am . . .
The dusty cover of the book, never read
The wilting petals of a thirsty flower
The flickering light bulb in the blackened room
The broken windowpane

I am . . .
The stub of a pencil
A torn up picture
The three legged chair in the corner
The missing piece of an unfinished jigsaw.

Elizabeth Wright (12)
The Ecclesbourne School

Sunset

The sun's melting into the murky water
Trying to escape the glow of the moon.
The waves are erupting, crashing on ragged rocks,
Covering them with its watery cape,
Making them vanish behind a veil of spray.
The white horses are leaping out of the water,
Pawing at my ankles, encouraging me to play.
Wind is rushing through me, like a train on its rails.
This is my ideal holiday,
I wish I could stay for another day.

Mark Shepherd (12)
The Ecclesbourne School

Tired I Ams

I am
The old rusty car, spluttering on the drive.
The light bulb, flickering and dying.
The ancient television, wavering in and out of focus.
The computer on the desk, running out of memory.
The clock on the mantelpiece, hands moving slower as the battery
runs out.
I am
The pair of scuffed shoes, with laces fraying.
The shopping bag in the cupboard, handles beginning to snap.
The white cushion on the settee, starting to go flat.
The T-shirt worn so many times, the colours are all fading.
The winter scarf in the wardrobe, beginning to unravel.
I am
The black plastic biro, running out of ink.
The reading book, pages yellowing, black ink turning grey.
The silver scissors, going blunt, starting to lose their shine.
The multicoloured children's paints, starting to dry up.
The pack of cards, bought years ago, whose corners are
starting to curl.
I am
The muddy-brown football, wheezing as it deflates.
The bolt on the front door, rusting, getting stiff.
The notice board, near the Church Hall, paint beginning to peel.
The once cream carpet, in the hall, downtrodden and covered in mud.
The historic building, going to ruin, corners starting to crumble.
Tired I am.

Rosalyn Smith (12)
The Ecclesbourne School

In A Field

A pheasant emerges, wings spread wide,
Cries of laughter in the summer sun,
Bounding through tufts of long grass,
Tail wagging, ears flopping.
The dog chases his stick.

James Smith (11)
The Ecclesbourne School

Newcomer

Sitting there all alone
Just sitting
People stare as they walk by,
They laugh and say,
'Who is it?'
They just stare as if I'm from another planet

Is it my hair?
Is it my facial features?
Is it the way I dress?
Is it how I stand?
Am I really that different?

We're all here for the same reason
So why are they treating me as if I'm different?
We're all made up the same
So why do they treat me as if I'm strange?

Just one more lesson to go
The day is nearly done,
Can't wait to get home
Where I feel I belong,
Maybe tomorrow will be different.

Rosie Dodd (12)
The Hucknall National School

Summer

An ice cream season,
A seaside prison,
A time for holidays,
A life of Sundays,
That's what summer means to me.

Warm evenings,
Lots of seeings,
Summer parties,
Sweets and Smarties,
That's what summer means to me.

Hot sunshine, cream teas,
Trees swaying in the breeze.
Climbing high to see the view,
I love summer, you should too.

Matthew Burton (12)
The Hucknall National School

I Lost My Best Friend Today

I lost my best friend today,
with her red hair and dark brown eyes.
I lost my best friend today
when she played and listened to me.
I lost my best friend today
with her sulky moods and curly ears.
I lost my best friend today,
If found please return, she's a much loved dog.

Alison Stones (13)
The Hucknall National School

The Fog

When I walk outside I start to shiver,
I look at my breath and it makes me wither.
I cannot see and I start to dither.
The fog!

I rub my hands together.
I hope for better weather soon,
No more mysterious gloom.
The fog!

Standing at the bus stop,
Shivering now and then,
Hope the bus comes soon,
It's nearly half-past ten.
The fog!

Now the day has ended,
It's time to go home.
The fog has disappeared.
Now the sun is shining bright,
It's a wonderful sight.
The sunshine!

Georgia Noon (12)
The Hucknall National School

The Playground

A cold tarmac field of merriment,
A place where most children dedicate a period of their time to,
A dark field scattered through one third of the school,
A place in which some adults come into
And walk out with just memories of their childhood.

Allan Ndiweni (11)
The Hucknall National School

Sport For All

Sport for all, sport for all,
That's what we cheer when we kick our ball.
Sport makes you fit
When we put on our kit.
Using our energy,
Every time we hit.

Sport calms us down
And it has been found to get your heart racing.
It's worthwhile to step up the pacing,
So think of this when you run round town.

Live life to the full and answer the call,
Never been seen in a kit before,
Don't be a couch potato,
Start now, sooner than later.
Sport for all, sport for all.

Isabel Roe (12)
The Hucknall National School

Carefully

Carefully the mouse treads
Carefully her sense of smell spreads.
Carefully her feet patter,
Carefully she thinks about this matter.

Carefully she's weary about her home,
Carefully she goes and hides without a moan.
Carefully she's cautious, curious to find
A nice careful owner who is
Very kind!

Natalie Jowett (15)
The Hucknall National School

On My Skateboard

When I'm on my skateboard
I go really crazy.
One minute after, I'm seeing
Mr Praisy,
Then I get off it
And then I run around.
I do a drop off
And land on the ground.
People keep asking other
People, why the kerb
Had all this white stuff on?
They thought it was a nerd.
But really what it was,
Was me on my skateboard.

Daniel Walton (11)
The Hucknall National School

Just A Kid

I ain't got a girlfriend,
But I've got loads of friends.
All I care about is sports and other stuff.
I couldn't stress enough.

All I care about is being a kid,
I'm not an old man, I don't need to bid.
I don't want to grow up too fast,
I don't want to think about my past.

All my friends think that I'm sad,
But I'm not, I'm just not mad.
I don't wanna be a bad boy,
I don't wanna be treated like a toy.

Jacob Cole (11)
The Hucknall National School

My Dad

Beer belly
Watching telly,
That's what my dad is.

Football crazy
Very lazy
That's what my dad is.

Iron rejecter
Behaviour lecturer
That's what my dad is.

Games player
Bed layer
That's what my dad is.

Even though he's very mad,
I still love my dad.

Lucie Mann (12)
The Hucknall National School

A Football Is . . .

A football is . . .
A glory maker
A goal shaker
A leather sphere
Flies into tears.
A boot kicker
An accuracy picker
An Arsenal winner.
A Derby killer
A ninety minute sport,
Which takes a lot of thought.
My Life.

James Duncan (13)
The Hucknall National School

The Seasons In The Garden

Springtime:
Spring is the time when flowers grow, and the
lawn you must start to mow.
Spring is the time when the birds start their nests,
and we must make our garden look its best.

Summertime:
Summer is the time when the garden is in full flower,
the days are hot and long with only the odd shower.
Summer is the time for the special barbecues,
and when the days inside are few.

Autumn time:
Autumn is the time when the wind will blow,
And we must eat our garden vegetables to make us grow.
Autumn is the time when the trees go brown,
and all the leaves end up on the ground.

Wintertime:
Winter is the time when the snow covers the ground,
And when Mr Robin can be found.
Winter is the time when the garden is at rest,
waiting for springtime to look its best.

Jessica Padmore (11)
The Hucknall National School

My Books Are . . .

A place to escape to when things turn bad,
Another world; somebody else's life.
Dreams and fantasy in imagination's eye,
A fountain of knowledge for me to embrace.
It is something to look forward to whenever I like,
Finally, they keep me wondering, day and night.

Imogen Fearon (11)
The Hucknall National School

Scared

The drip of the tap
The squeak of the door,
The howl of the wind
The creak of the floor.

The hiss of the pipes,
The shadows of trees.
The crackle of fire
The click of my knees.

My teeth start to chatter,
I shiver with cold,
My hands start to shake
But I need to be bold.

The clock strikes twelve,
As I creep past.
I dash to my mum.
Safe at last.

Jodie Holmes (11)
The Hucknall National School

An Autumn Poem

Dark brown is the river,
Golden is the sand.
It flows along forever,
With trees on either hand.

Green leaves a-floating
Castles of the loam,
Old boats are boating.

Where will their journeys roam?

Ashleigh Taylor (12)
The Hucknall National School

Stolen

Stolen, stolen
Probably in a witch's cauldron,
Take it, break it,
Snatch it, snatch it.
Stolen, stolen,
Probably in a witch's cauldron.
'Rabble, babble,' the witches' words,
Back into their hands
You are banned.

Always broken,
But never spoken,
Gets lost.
Did you know how much that cost?
Stolen, stolen,
Probably in a witch's cauldron.
Speak out, tell the truth, never steal,
Show the world how you feel.

Laura Grace Marshall (11)
The Hucknall National School

Bored . . .

Staring at four walls
No one about,
Nobody calls,
Bored.

Daydreaming all day long,
Nothing to do,
Everything's going wrong.
Bored!
Just bored . . .

Jaide Croll (11)
The Hucknall National School

The Squirrel

I look out of the window and see a squirrel running
up and down the bird table, collecting nuts for the winter.

I look at him for a minute, I turn round and
look again, he's nowhere to be seen.

I love wildlife so, so much, that they keep coming
back for more, more nuts.

Squirrels are cute, squirrels are bushy, squirrels are
so, so clever and funny.

Every day I put things out for them,
the squirrels eat them, but I hope they
save some for the other birds.

Melissa Smith (11)
The Hucknall National School

Love

Love smells like freshly cut roses,
on a Saturday morning.

Love feels like a soft brown teddy bear,
with a pink and white nose.

Love tastes like a double chocolate gateaux,
with cream on top.

Love looks like a field of hearts,
none broken or sad.

Love sounds like a heartbeat,
in the soul of my chest.

Kealey Ashcroft (11)
The Hucknall National School

Of Those Hungered Who Search

And oh how we seek, running through the place,
We lost your path long ago; we lost your face.
And the darkness consumes us as we hide our faces
And shut out your light,
It guides us
But the darkness, the evil, it binds us.
We are hungry, thirsting,
For we all have to eat but how can we at your table?
How can we even take crumbs from the floor?
So I further myself and lock this door.
I can hardly remember it now -
But I'm sure there was a time when things weren't this way.
My eyes have gone bad, my body transparent.
I made no sound but the footsteps of my running away.
I'm drowning in myself, or is it the sea?
A sea of blood, pain and tears.
Crystal tears,
And no! I can't see the weights that hold me down.
I surrender; I drown.
It's not the same looking for something to hold on to
So I don't fall away.
It's not the same when I fall into the way I was before.
It's not the same, yet my heart still fails me, again.
I press harder, my face into my hands, to hide the shame
I know I have,
Then you cause me to breathe in more of you. more!
Oh when do I come back to you?
Oh, let me in.
The door has been opened by your blood,
Here I am . . .
Find me, place me in your hand.
So when do I come back to you?
When can I bask in your presence?
When can I see your face?
Forgiven . . .
Let us feast.

Tim Maiden (15)
The Hucknall National School

Did You Ever See?

Did you ever see the sky so blue?
Did you ever see the grass so green?
Did you ever see the world so black?
Did you ever see so many dead?
No! I did. I saw it.

Did you ever hear so much silence?
Did you ever hear so many screams?
Did you ever hear so many shots?
Did you ever hear people pleading for their lives?
No! I did. I heard it.

Did you ever feel so cold?
Did you ever feel so unloved?
Did you ever feel so much hatred?
Did you ever feel so alone?
No! I did. I felt it.

Did you ever touch the sky?
Did you ever touch a dead person?
Did you ever touch a warm hand?
Did you ever touch a gun?
No! I did. I touched it.

Did you ever taste so much gas?
Did you ever taste blood?
Did you ever taste the salt in the sea?
Did you ever taste the hatred between two people?
No! I did. I tasted it.

Did you ever dream of a world at peace?
Did you ever dream of no violence?
Did you ever dream of death?
Did you ever dream of love?
No! I did, I dreamed it.

Victoria Kirkpatrick (14)
The Hucknall National School

She's Gone

Her grip loosens
As I try to hold on tight
She's trembling with fear
I'm trying with all my might.

I can't believe it
My best friend's about to fall
I hate the way good things become bad
In fact, I hate it all.

Any minute she could let go
And I would never forgive myself
Nothing could ever replace her
Not presents, fame or wealth.

Her hands are wet with sweat
She's gradually slipping away
I don't want to lose her
It's a terrible price to pay.

My hands suddenly feel lighter
And in horror I let out a cry
She couldn't hold on any longer
My best mate's in the sea, about to die.

Tears stream down my cheeks
As I call out her name
My own voice echoes back to me
And I know that life will never be the same.

Nicola Maiden (13)
The Hucknall National School

Haiku Poem - School

At nine forty-five
The bell rings in both my ears
Now school has started.

The smell of polish,
On the squeaky clean new floor
Is thrown up my nose.

As I enter art,
Paints glisten in their pallets
Waiting to be used.

Time for geography,
Where we read from a textbook,
Looking at some maps.

And after, it's maths,
Trying to do Algebra
Until lunch, at last!

Then games looms ahead,
Playing netball in the rain,
I hope that I score!

And lastly, it's science,
Learning about chemicals
Waiting for the bell.

The end of the day!
I catch my bus and I sigh,
Good job it's Friday!

Ruth Goodwin (12)
The Hucknall National School

Love Is . . .

Love is heart warming,
tummy churning,
belly turning.
I love being loved.

Love is a beautiful feeling,
heart healing,
love has a meaning.
I love being loved.

Hollie Jackson (12)
The Hucknall National School

Little Bunny

Fluffy, cuddly,
White fur ruffling,
Little bunny.

Cotton-ball tail,
Small red eyes.

Thumping, jumping,
White fur ruffling,
Little bunny.

Rhianne Poole (11)
The Hucknall National School

Star

Life is like a star
Shining so brightly
But when the next night comes
And it's not there
You know it will still be
Shining brightly, somewhere.

Laura Callan (14)
The Meadows Community School

Life Is Like . . .

Life is like a river,
A rush of pounding water.
Life is like a digitless clock,
Never-ending, it doesn't seem to stop.
A pendulum, swinging backwards
And forwards with its ups and downs.
Life is like a path,
You go down one, you come right back!

Life is also similar to a beautiful vase,
However fragile and often broken.
When a black sheet of dark, grey matter
Engulfs us in darkness.
People say death is lonely, dark and sad,
But what if death is bright, colourful and peaceful -
When the pendulum or digitless clock stops?

People never know
So they just keep wondering.
So I think I'll keep on thinking and wondering.
What life is really like!

Karl Boulton (14)
The Meadows Community School

Homeless

They live alone, upon the streets,
With no one there for comfort,
But their thumping heartbeats.
But who can blame them for what they do,
Is this the life for me and you?
Would you be able to look after a child
When you're only one yourself?
Their faces look so withered and wild,
But there is life behind that tortured face,
It's just waiting for the time and the place.

Richard Hancock (14)
The Meadows Community School

Changes

Changes are all about life,
And as one ends, another begins.
It is like a mixture which keeps repeating itself,
Every single year.
The first change is where life begins
For the newly formed.
Where colour fills the dark and dull.
It is a happy time for the living,
In the rain and in the sun.
As this change dies, another occurs.
The sun decides to stay out for longer hours
And the days go on and on.
Another form of life comes out to play,
As it is the favourite change of the year.
But life gets worse for every living thing
As the next change forms and the favourite ends.
Life begins to die back down and begins to turn orange and gold,
This change is beautiful but it's the start of the end.
When the final change arrives all living things are
Either dead or asleep.
The change is also very beautiful,
As a gleaming white cover usually comes out at this time.
Even though it is a sad change in life,
There is always excitement for the next change to happen.

Michael Clarke (14)
The Meadows Community School

Something's Changed, Something's Changed

In the old house
Where she used to live,
Something's changed
Something's gone.

There's that old chair
Where she used to sit,
Something's changed
Something's gone.

There's that old TV,
That she used to watch,
Something's changed
Something's gone.

She stood there
But now she's not,
She's changed
She's gone.

Gemma Ord (14)
The Meadows Community School

Haunted Life

Transparent thoughts
Drift through air
Yet no one notices
Her life lay bare.

Some may love her
Some may care
But it's her life
Drifting there.

Tom Millington (14)
The Meadows Community School

The Rising Sun

Beginning to clear,
making way
for the magical sun
to come out to play.

Gleaming through
tightly held clouds,
the bright orange ray
beaming down.

Reflecting on the
wonderful flowers,
using all its great powers.

By day it's here,
by night it's gone,
rising and falling
until it disappears.

Gemma Brockington (15)
The Meadows Community School

Two Sides

One was rich, one was poor,
One can't be bothered,
One wants more.
One will fight, one will run,
One will work,
One had fun.

Two sides to every story,
But you need them both.
To determine who's the real winner
And who deserves the gold.

Amy Newbold (14)
The Meadows Community School

There!

It sits there at night, still quiet,
The moonlit sky reflects upon it.
All the stars seem to fall in it,
The clouds appear to be sitting on it

It reflects the light, captures the sky,
It glistens on anything that passes by.
It says not a word, just sits there still,
Look tomorrow. Be there? It will!

It never goes
It always stays,
There in the night
There again in the day.

Some say it's pretty,
Like a giant mirror.
But me personally . . .
I call it a river.

Jodie Millan (14)
The Meadows Community School

The Ocean

The beautiful scenery,
The stunning landscape of the ocean,
The waves crashing against the rocks.
The foam of the water
Splashes up in the air.

As the sun goes down,
The sea goes out.
It slowly goes silent,
And the crashing is no more.

Daniel Hawkins (14)
The Meadows Community School

Riding A Bike

One winding path,
Eyes that look down
To see a wheel.
A grey haired figure
Arms out wide.
Waiting to catch me
As I go, side to side.

I close my eyes
Just for a second,
Dare I open them? No!
I'm on my own!
Nobody to help me.
What do I do?
I don't know, I can't see.

A rush of wind
Through my hair,
Count to three
And open my eyes.
Everything's a blur.
I laugh and giggle,
I can't believe it -
I can ride, but I daren't wriggle.

Sarah Stones (14)
The Meadows Community School

The Love Chain

Love is like a golden chain
That links our hearts together
And if you ever break that chain
You'll break my heart forever.

Joanna Farrar (14)
The Meadows Community School

The Freaky Freezer

Oh no, it's got me,
It's sucking me in.
It wants to freeze me
And feed on my skin.

I'm halfway in,
I'm beginning to freeze,
I feel all numb
And I can't feel my knees.

I grab hold of the hoover
And shout for help,
And the hoover turns round and laughs.
I do nothing but yelp.

I've got nothing to do
But hope for the best.
It starts to squeeze me,
I hear cracking from my chest.

I struggle to breathe,
I'm gonna die,
But then my mum comes
And turns on the light.

Daniel Allen (12)
The Meadows Community School

Life

One huge emotion that follows
You through life,
That will always ask you
If you had just done right.

But as long as you achieve
What you set out to see,
Then no one can tell you
Who you should or shouldn't be!

Lindsey Keller (14)
The Meadows Community School

My Perfect Day

The sun gleaming on my perfect day,
The birds singing on my perfect day.
The flowers dancing on my perfect day.
The grass swaying on my perfect day.
The fields coming alive on my perfect day.
The air perfumed on my perfect day.
The people congregated on my perfect day.
Competing at sport on my perfect day.
People cheering on my perfect day.
Running on my perfect day.
Going and competing in the Olympics on my perfect day,
Crossing the finishing line first on my perfect day.
Collecting gold on my perfect day.
Being a star on my perfect day.
Meeting Kelly Holmes on my perfect day.

Abbie Vernon (12)
The Meadows Community School

My Perfect Day

Lovely sunny day stretching before me,
Emotions whizzing around inside,
Smells wafting on the breeze,
Ice cream, candyfloss, giraffe dung, elephant wee.

Parrots squawking, lions roaring,
Can I make the sounds the monkeys do?
Chop the carrots, peel the bananas,
Spoon the Calpol, hide the vitamin tablets.

Gorillas need toys and things to do,
Sweeping, scrubbing, plenty of work for me.
Fascinating facts, lots of learning,
Wish all the school days were as exciting.

Kathryn Smith (12)
The Meadows Community School

The First Day Of Year 7

First day of Year 7 was quite OK,
But there were a few rules we had to obey.
Not to chew, not to run, but to walk,
Not to eat with our fingers, but with a knife and fork.

When I first got there it didn't seem right,
All the older ones gave me a fright.
They all seemed to tower over me,
I heard something knocking, it was my knees.

Some of the teachers were quite nice,
But for some we had to be as quiet as mice.
If we weren't, we'd get detention,
Where you get no attention.

Some lessons I just don't like, they are oh so boring,
We just sit there, listening to the teacher roaring.
When we finally do some work it's time to pack away.
'Hooray, hooray,' we all shout, 'we've survived our first day.'

Kerry Ford (12)
The Meadows Community School

The Rainbow Colours

T-shirt is red
Ice lolly is orange,
Sunflower is yellow
Sky is blue,
Jumper is indigo
And the plants in the park
Are a violet colour.

Glen Chui (14)
The Meadows Community School

Hallowe'en

H allowe'en is here,
A time we all fear,
L ollies, sugar, sherbet and choc,
L et's give the neighbours a shock.
O gres hide behind a tree,
W aiting to scare you or me,
E ven ghosts waiting to jump,
E verywhere monsters that will make our hearts thump.
N ight-time is here, so let's go to bed and pull the quilt over our head.

Lauren Marsden (12)
The Meadows Community School

Burning Love

Love is like a candle
It brightly burns away
Who knows how long the flame will last
How long the love will stay?

It's started by a single spark
Then love begins to grow
But will the love be snatched away
Or will the flame still glow?

Donna Barnett (14)
The Meadows Community School

You And Me

The stars are shining very bright,
They're like the twinkle in your eyes.
You and me for evermore,
We're like a handle, stuck to a door.
We're tied together like a dog on a lead
Till death do us part,
Forever we'll be.

Natasha Louise Taylor (14)
The Meadows Community School

My Perfect Poem

A day of fun, laughter and happiness.

D reaming night whispers and stirring,
A day to do as I please,
Y elling, shouting on and off.

T ime, not a flicker of it gone, not passed me by,
O n the settee, so cosy and warm.

R aces, on a go-kart, not a care,
E mpty streets, to do as I dare,
M ore sweets to munch, more biscuits to crunch,
E very step is another I make,
M oving on a board of air in my mind,
B ehaviour isn't a problem, it's all deserted,
E choes of my voice, nothing to drown me,
R emember my chance of a lifetime.

Mitchell Royle (12)
The Meadows Community School

First Day Of School

On the 1st September,
I'm back at school,
All new friends and
I feel like a fool.

It's twenty-past twelve,
Time for dinner,
I'm feeling quite hungry,
Just hope there isn't liver.

It's fifth period,
Ten minutes to go,
Tons of homework,
Only thirty-nine weeks to go.

Ryan Clark (13)
The Meadows Community School

My Perfect Day

My perfect day would be
Going to a place abroad,
That's hot and has palm trees
Swaying in the island breeze.

Tropical and exotic fruits,
Hot and white sandy beaches,
Clear blue and crystal seas,
Learning to surf - in Hawaii.

Sleeping in a king-sized bed,
In a five star hotel,
Having my hair and nails done
In a LA salon.

But there's only one thing
That would make my day perfect,
And that would be for my best friend, Lauren,
To spend my day with me.

Eleanor Couch (12)
The Meadows Community School

Dawn Is Coming

Dawn is coming,
anxious I get.
Nobody there
in silence, I stare.
Excited and amazed
loving the time.
Like the experience
enjoying waiting for
dawn to come.

Tyne Hadley (14)
The Meadows Community School

The Wardrobe

The wardrobe's door creaked,
Dark shadows moved all around,
The dust smelled like something had leaked,
The old fashioned wardrobe wouldn't calm down.

The doors swayed open,
I was forced inside,
It locked me in and boxed me in,
I wanted to run and hide.

While I was in the darkness,
It started to move around,
I heard lots of banging noises,
And other scary sounds.

It moved quite a long distance,
As far as I could tell,
Then it fell forward,
It was like going to Hell.

Then there was a crash
And a screech from far away,
It felt like a fearful clash,
I suddenly began to pray.

Amber Kimberley Staples (12)
The Meadows Community School

My Mars Bar

Not a Freddo, not that cheap,
You're dark, mysterious, and you're deep.
Not a Yorkie, not for girls,
You are a Mars bar, the best in the world.
You don't show emotions because you are tough,
But I know you are as soft as fluff.
As much as I like you and think you are great,
You don't compare to an After Eight.

Chris Childs (13)
The Meadows Community School

My Hoover

My hoover is magic,
Sucking up everything in sight.
It likes to eat everything that's about,
But I bet you can't guess what
Its favourite meal can be?
When it's hungry, it sucks up *me!*

As it sleeps,
I try to keep still,
With every footstep I take,
Make sure it doesn't awake.

As it wakes,
I try to take a chance,
But I can't move around,
I can't make a sound.

Jade Ryan (12)
The Meadows Community School

Silence

There she is,
Sat in the corner.
There she is,
All on her own.
There they are,
Teasing and taunting her.
There she is,
Crying alone.
There I am,
Not helping, or caring,
But when tomorrow comes
There she won't be.
Where will she be?
She'll be gone.

Lauri Smith (14)
The Meadows Community School

Life

Life is little,
Life is long,
Why lavish it
On something wrong?

Life is fast,
Life is slow,
Why lavish it
On making a foe?

Life is gripping,
Life is dull,
Why lavish it
If it can be full?

Life is old,
Why pretend?
You are young
Until the end.

Joe Hawkins (13)
The Meadows Community School

So Big, Yet So Small

Big kids to the left,
Big kids to the right,
All of them giving me a fright.
Friends of the family shouting, 'Hello',
Introducing themselves to people they don't know.
Making new friends, not on my own,
Swapping numbers in our phones.
So small, yet so big,
In my new secondary school.

Layonie Rawson (12)
The Meadows Community School